Praise for

I STILL WANT TO BE AN
ASTRONAUT

"They say it takes talent, good looks, charisma, and a solid work ethic to be successful in life—but James and I are proof that you don't really need any of those."
—JOHN BYTHEWAY, best-selling author and public speaker

"I can tell James tried really hard."
—NATALIE MADSEN, Studio C actor, regional Emmy Award-winning writer, and UFC Fighter

"Writing a good book is difficult, as this one clearly demonstrates."
—MATT MEESE, Studio C actor

"Words, sentences, paragraphs, even punctuation! This book has it all!"
—The Letter H just looking for a good time

"This book is better than the movie! The movie being *Transformers 4*."
—ADAM BERG, Studio C actor and author of *Death of the Psychopomp*

"This has changed my life! I see things so much more clearly now!"
—Overheard at a LASIK center

"I've read this book multiple times! Everyone should buy it!"
—JAMES PERRY, Studio C actor and author of *I Still Want to Be an Astronaut*

I STILL WANT TO BE AN
ASTRONAUT

Living Your Dream When You Dream Too Much

JAMES PERRY

CFI

An imprint of Cedar Fort, Inc.
Springville, Utah

ISBN 13: 978-1-4621-2288-2

Published by CFI, an imprint of Cedar Fort, Inc.
2373 W. 700 S., Springville, UT 84663
Distributed by Cedar Fort, Inc., www.cedarfort.com

LIBRARY OF CONGRESS CATALOGING-IN-PUBLICATION DATA

Names: Perry, James, 1987- author.
Title: I still want to be an astronaut : living your dream when you dream too
    much / James Perry.
Description: Springville, Utah : CFI, an imprint of Cedar Fort, Inc., [2018]
    | Includes bibliographical references and index.
Identifiers: LCCN 2018034818 (print) | LCCN 2018040193 (ebook) | ISBN
    9781462129607 (epub, pdf, mobi) | ISBN 9781462122882 (perfect bound : alk.
    paper)
Subjects: LCSH: Self-actualization (Psychology) | Self-realization. | Perry,
    James, 1987- | LCGFT: Autobiographies.
Classification: LCC BF637.S4 (ebook) | LCC BF637.S4 P4445 2018 (print) | DDC
    158--dc23
LC record available at https://lccn.loc.gov/2018034818

Cover design by Jeff Harvey
Cover design © 2018 Cedar Fort, Inc.
Edited by Kathryn Watkins and Sydnee Hyer
Typeset by Kaitlin Barwick

Printed in the United States of America

10 9 8 7 6 5 4 3 2 1

Printed on acid-free paper

To my lovely wife, who is the reason for
most good things in my life.
I love you. Just a normal amount.

And to my daughter, June. I hope something here helps you on your
journey when you stop rebelling and just read my book.
You are the light of my life.

Oh, and to whatever other kids I might have,
you are also the lights of my life.

Contents

CONTENTS

Introduction

I don't really like introductions, because I want to get right into the meat of the book, but it always feels like I have to get through the introduction in case I miss anything. So, this introduction is over.

You're welcome. Enjoy this picture of my greatest outfit ever.

Introducing You to the Book

But This Is Totally Not an Introduction

as·tro·naut

/ˈas-trə-ˌnȯt/

noun

1. A general term used to express what someone wants to be when they grow up.

Origin

From the Greek *astro*, meaning "boring," and *naut*, which is just a weird way to spell *not*, combined to mean "not boring."

Example

"I want to be an astronaut when I grow up, unlike that boring job my dad has."

synonyms: Fireman, princess, famous, guy who gets paid to eat ice cream.

College was both the hardest time in my life and the most fun I had ever had.

I married my high school sweetheart, Brenna, the summer before my sophomore year, and she is the most fun person I know. A year later, I got into Divine Comedy and made good friends doing sketch comedy for sold-out audiences. I got into the mechanical engineering program and was stoked to be learning the most interesting things in science and math, because I am a hardcore nerd.

But I was also freaking out. I worried so much about my future and the future of my family. I didn't know what my purpose in life was, and I felt so much pressure to figure it out. If I didn't, I would be wasting my time on the wrong thing, only to become terrible at my job and completely miserable in general life. I would spend my days crying until one rainy Tuesday when I would come home to find my dog standing on the front porch with a suitcase in paw, shaking his head as he got into an Uber and drove off, fading into the distance, never to be seen again. I cry a single tear; the last one I have left.

The thing is, my life isn't the 1993 hit comedy *Groundhog Day*, featuring Bill Murray and Andie MacDowell, where you get infinite chances to try again until you get it right. If I blow a thousand dollars on a half-hour piano lesson, I will still suck at piano *and* I'm out a thousand dollars.

So I worried a lot about what to do with my life, and I'm guessing you do too, because you're reading this book. Or maybe you're reading it because you saw the cover and thought, "That looks like an intelligent human being right there. Let's see what he has to say."

Do you ever wonder what your purpose in life is? Do you ever feel regret or hopelessness about ever finding the right thing or being the right person? Do you ever wish you were someone else? Do you poop out of parties?

I did, and my journey has taught me some lessons I wish I had known earlier. This book is my best attempt at sharing those lessons. I hope something here can help you get a little closer to living your dream.

Don't worry. I'm not going to tell you how to live *my* dream. This is about figuring out your own dream. However, I do have this theory, similar to *The Truman Show,* but different. My life is really a super high-tech virtual reality video game that my spirit is playing, and when I die, it's game over. I go back to heaven and play a different life game, and someone else can play "James Perry Life." I mean, when you have eternity, it makes sense that games would be 100 years long (which is how long I plan to live. No need to set a record. Oldest Person Alive is also a popular heaven arcade game, I imagine).

But I can honestly say my life is such a dream that I could see it being a highly rated arcade game. So, how did I get here? What's my secret? What did I *do*?

My story isn't all that amazing on paper; I was really just an average guy, good at some things, bad at others. The transformation wasn't mind-blowing, like a drug-addicted felon who completed rehab and became a yoga instructor and dog rescuer. But it felt just as mind-blowing as that to me. If you're just an average person hoping for a life that your current self would envy, that's enough to make the change worth it. We're not trying to impress anyone here. We just want to live a great life we can be proud of.

LIVING THE DREAM

So, like I said, my life is a dream, but not in the way you might think.

We call our hopes and ambitions "dreams" because dreams are wonderful and magical and full of surprises. Your imagination can soar (and so can you if you know how to control your dreams, which I don't, sadly). Dreams come with a promise of fulfillment and a better you.

This is where most people stop when they think of dreams. But dreams are also weird, and sometimes scary, and not fully in your control. Dreams can make you wonder if protecting your family from Brad Pitt biting their heads off should be a real concern. But one thing is consistent through every dream: It is completely, uniquely *yours*. Unless I've successfully passed that Brad Pitt nightmare on to you. You're welcome.

I believe living a life that is completely *yours* is a far greater goal than living a life that is "perfect" or "great" or even "happy." Those goals often lead to failure, because they require you to rid yourself of the weird, scary, and unruly parts of life, which is useless and even counterproductive, because they are necessary parts of life. You're much more likely to *feel* perfect, great, or happy when you learn to love the uncomfortable parts of life.

This book is about living your dream life. It's about the journey of figuring out what to do with your future while living your life to the fullest now. I'll tell you about my journey and what I've learned. You might think, "James, you're not a psychologist or advanced academic. What gives you the right to teach me anything?" I may not be a psychologist, but I played a guy seeing a psychologist on TV. So, you tell me.

I have a PhD in James! Man, I wish I had a gif right now. I hate that gifs don't work in books. They're so good at expressing mood. GIF: Guy with one hand on his hip and the other giving a "thumbs up." Goofy smile. Over and over.

Still don't think I'm qualified? I got a bachelor's degree in mechanical engineering, so I can solve all the equations and design specialty wrenches. I can haz be smart enough from *that*? Yes? Good.

If you're a fan of Studio C, I'll do my utmost to talk smack about my fellow cast members.

Wherever I can, I back up my advice with quotes and research, such as Harvard. I read other books and steal their ideas, because I have a page count minimum.

I consider myself to be living my dream life. People who know me from my work on Studio C probably aren't surprised to hear that. My job is fun . . . usually. But that isn't the whole picture, because it's not all roses and butterflies or whatever the saying is. It's not all cookies and pedicures, people. There are days that are terrible, rough, lonely, long, cold, considerably deleterious, etc. Not just at work. My wife, Brenna, and my daughter, June, are the best wife and daughter a guy can have. But it's not all snow days and baby butts. Life is tough sometimes, even in my dream life. So why do I call it a dream life? It's wonderful and scary, magical and unruly, full of surprises both good and bad. But, it's completely, uniquely *mine*.

Well, most of the time. When I do things the way I'm supposed to, when I follow the principles I talk about in this book, I get close to the ultimate goal of making my life *mine*, and the good and the bad come together in beautiful unity. You were built to be happy and successful, and you just need to get out of your own way. Make life truly yours, and you won't wish you were anyone else.

So, who should read this book? This book is for you if:

- You struggle to decide what to do with your life, and you want to make the right decision.
- You've decided what to do, but you're wondering if it was the right choice.
- You want to live life to the fullest (whether you've decided what to do with your life or not).
- You like fun books.
- You like me.
- You dislike me (I'll either change your mind or solidify it).
- You wear colorful socks.
- You genuinely want to listen to people, but you find yourself halfway through their story and you have no idea what they have been saying, so you nod and say, "Right." (I know a lot about this. You're not alone, and you're still a good friend . . . in other ways.)
- You're Charlize Theron and you want to get to know me a little before you put me in your next movie.

What this book won't do:

- Teach you how to be an actual spaceman astronaut
- Teach you how to control your actual sleeping dreams (someone write that book and send it to me)
- Do your chores for you (someone write that book and send it to me)
- Read your mind
- Take over humanity and say with an evil grin, "Looks like the shoe is on the other foot!" To which, Rick replies, "It would have been better if you said, 'The other footnote!'" Rick is immediately executed.

There are plenty of things this book can't do, but we're going to focus on what it can do. Just like there are plenty of things *you* can't do, but we're going to focus on what you can do.

GIF: Guy with one hand on his hip and the other giving a "thumbs up." Goofy smile. Over and over.

I use that GIF a lot.

DON'T BE PAVLOV'S DOG

Some guy named Pavlov did a famous experiment where he rang a bell every time he fed his dog. Because Fido associated the bell with food, he became conditioned to salivate when he heard the bell, even when there was no food in sight. You are also conditioned to respond a certain way to things that happen to you. Someone insults you, you get offended. Something costs more than you thought, you feel robbed. You see your brother is wearing your shirt, you immediately get angry and start pulling it off his body. I'm sorry, Greg; I admit now that I overreacted.

Everything in this book is about taking a step back and noticing your reactions to things, then trying new ways of reacting that are purposeful and driven by your choice to live your dream life. You can change the way you react to things so you are not a victim of what happens to you. Someone insults you, maybe you kiss them. Something costs more than you thought, you think of all the generosity people have shown you and trust that you will be always be taken care of. You see your brother wearing your shirt, you get angry and start pulling if off his body, but *gently* this time instead of hitting him. Baby steps.

There's a universe outside your window that you have barely discovered, and it requires you to break out of your conditioning. Just like the universe, you have endless potential. You just have to go beyond your own little world to see it, and when you see it from higher up, you remind yourself of how beautiful it really is. Don't be like Pavlov's dog; be like my dog, Caesar, who apparently can't be conditioned and just prances around to his heart's content regardless of what I say.

In the next chapter, I explain how I went from abundant stress and confusion to living an abundant, happy life. Finding your purpose goes beyond a great job. It includes everything you do with your time: relationships, volunteering, money, aforementioned prancing, and so on. If this book leads to you figuring out your one dream job, fantastic. But if it doesn't, maybe your path will be like mine and lead you to multiple dream jobs that you don't even know about right now. What I hope it leads to is finding purpose and feeling like you really matter, that you contribute in your own way, and that's the only way to do anything. You can be living your dream life and still dream about what might be next. After all, I still want to be an astronaut.

How I Became a Professional Absurdsman

I've always had a hard time figuring out where I fit in the scheme of things. What do I want to do? Who do I want to be? It's like a square-peg-in-a-round-hole situation, but worse. I've tried so many different things, it's more like I'm a weird, misshapen, octopus peg trying to fit into a rhomboid hole.

I'm jealous of people who just somehow knew, from a young age, what their purpose in life was. Elizabeth Gilbert, author of *Eat, Pray, Love*, always knew she wanted to be a writer, and she was very successful. Jennifer Lawrence said she always knew she was going to be famous. A lot of successful people talk about how they knew what they wanted and went for it, against all odds, and just kept going through the darkest days until they came out victorious.

I really wanted to have that kind of drive, to dedicate myself to something great and make a difference in the world. How did others know what they were doing was the right thing? How could I know for myself that I was doing the best I could with my time and talents? I didn't want to squander all of my effort on the wrong thing, so I needed to figure out what was my purpose in life. Then I could stop wasting time and money exploring different options.

I was really concerned about wasting time. The problem was, every minute I wasted doing something other than my purpose became stressful for me, because I equated wasting time with something horrendous like helpless puppies dying of something awful because I wasn't taking the time to save them. If I wasn't focused on my purpose, I felt like I was losing precious minutes. You can't enjoy binging Netflix with that thought in the back of your mind.

A lot of people get inspiration from quotes about not being lazy, getting your butt in gear, and how you have as many hours in a day as Beyoncé. Not me. Those quotes just add to my stress of already punishing myself for not using my precious moments to save those helpless puppies. I need the quotes that say, "What you are is good enough," or "If you swing and miss, God always pitches again," or simply, "Whatever you're doing right now, you're not murdering puppies." That's by far my favorite proverb.

I figured if other people knew what they wanted to do as child, then I should figure out what I loved and what I was good at when I was a child. So I asked my parents, "What did you notice about me?"

"Oh, you were reading books at a really young age."

Okay, that sounds like a smart person, maybe an academic. Go on.

"And you were so cuddly. You were our most cuddly boy. And you were always outside in the dirt; we couldn't get the dirt off of you, you were such a dirty little kid."

So, while other kids were dreaming of their futures and writing, "I want to be an astronaut when I grow up," I was eating dirt and being cuddly. Which, to be fair, is still how I spend about 50 percent of my time, but that conversation didn't help me figure out my purpose.

For a while I wondered if the only real cause of success is just hard work. Just pick anything and work hard enough and you can be great at it. But watch me play sports, and you will soon see that is wrong. The only thing I'm good at is getting hit in the head. Seriously, it's uncanny. It's almost magical. Even my friends know this is true, because it happens when I play sports with them. It is so much a part of me now that I almost feel like when it happens it's really God sending me a message, "Don't worry, James. You're still you, and I'm aware of you."

I'm so good at getting hit in the head, I don't even have to be playing the sport. Once we were at Jason Gray's house and everyone was playing ping pong. I had already gone down for the night, because I'm a seventy-year-old. The players and the crowd were energetic and loud, and I was on the couch just a few feet away, so I couldn't sleep and figured I would join them. No sooner did I sit down on the sidelines than one of the players hit the ball as hard as he could. If you've ever been hit by a ping pong ball, you know it actually hurts more than you think, from that little, super light, plastic ball. I wish it was the ball that hit me. Unfortunately, the player also let go of the paddle, which was traveling just as fast as the ball. Very irresponsible.

The paddle went straight to my forehead. Actually, given my track record, the paddle was probably flying in a different direction, saw my head, and decided I hadn't been reminded of God's love recently. It left a mark that looked like a tiny motorcycle skid, like Stuart Little made a sharp U-turn right on my forehead.

I solidly tried a few sports as a kid. I tried soccer, basketball, and volleyball. I didn't try baseball because of the head-magnet thing. That, I knew, would go very poorly. Though I did get hit in the head with a kickball. Yet here I am, multiple concussions later, worse at sports than when I started. No matter how hard you work, if you're a pair of scissors trying to cut grass, you'll never get as much done as a lawn mower. But the lawn mower can't get a big head, because no one would ever let him cut hair. Everyone has their strengths and weaknesses.

So, my first year of college, I changed my major from landscape management to philosophy to mathematics to journalism to mechanical engineering. Engineering fit pretty well, because I was good at math, I was interested in science, and it was a good mix of the two. Slowly, I was getting some answers and figuring out my purpose.

I needed a break from all this really practical purpose-finding, so I joined a comedy club on campus called Divine Comedy. It was a creative outlet for me that I didn't get from engineering. Don't get me wrong, I see beauty and art in math and science, but something about comedy and performance resonated with me deeply. Divine

Comedy changed my whole college career. Even though I was busier than before, I actually got more done in school because I had a creative outlet that let me reset my mind and gave me energy. I had so much fun and made life-long friends, and I couldn't get enough of it. But, of course, this was just goofing around and wasting time. I had to make sure I was still fulfilling my purpose and being useful to the world.

Divine Comedy led to the creation of Studio C, the family-friendly sketch comedy TV show where I currently work. At first, it was just a part-time gig. I graduated and got an engineering job full-time, but I also wore ridiculous glasses and talked about lobster bisque on the side. Then, something crazy happened.

The show had grown enough that they wanted to hire the cast full-time. I was being offered a real job as an actor, which I didn't think was possible for me. The question was, do I take time away from finding my purpose to go goof off for a couple years? Remember, I didn't do too well with wasting time (keep in mind the helpless puppies). But it was a once-in-a-lifetime opportunity, and it was a dream of mine, so I decided I could pause my purpose-finding and have some fun while I had the opportunity. Then, something even crazier happened.

We started getting letters from fans. Some said that in their darkest days, Studio C was the only thing that could cheer them up. Some said they were so happy they finally found clean, high-quality entertainment they could watch as a family. It almost started to seem like my dream job had purpose. Somehow, wasting time doing what I loved was helping other people be a little happier. This changed my whole perspective, because I realized I found more purpose in doing something that was important to me than in doing something that I assumed was important to the world.

It turns out my purpose wasn't found in obsessing about developing the right skills, but in developing the skills necessary to do what I was obsessed with.

So here it is. My secret. Ready? You have no purpose in life.

Don't assume you need to find your one true purpose in life and work only toward that one thing before you can do what you were meant to do. You are alive today, so you have purpose today. I believe any real method for finding purpose should give you immediate purpose, even if it's on your way to finding future purposes. That's right, purposes, with an *s*. That's the big change I want you to make in your mind.

When I say you have no purpose in life, I mean you don't have *one* purpose that rules all of your decisions. You don't have this grand, romanticized thing that is your "one purpose in life."

"Aww, man! I thought this book was going to help me figure out what job I should get."

It actually is, and in a much better way than forcing yourself to figure it out now. It may seem like you want to know your purpose, because you need to take the right classes and get into the right school so you can get the right training and fulfill your purpose in life. I hope I can get you to change your mind from always *trying* to do the right thing to always *doing* the true thing.

What on earth does that mean?

The true thing is being true to yourself, even a self that you don't fully know yet. It's being true to your situation and the people around you by recognizing your need for others. The right thing is what you are *supposed* to do, because you think someone requires it of you. The true thing is what you do *because it is who you are* and who you aspire to be.

I've got four tips for finding your purpose—things that would have relieved a lot of stress for me if I had known them early on. These tips even help me today, because I still think about what I might do next. Studio C is fantastic for now, but I might look awkward as sixty-year-old doing sketch comedy with all the twenty-year-old newcomers. And science still doesn't know how to make old people look young; I checked. They did a study on it called *Real Housewives*.

If I have to categorize them (and I do, because I'm writing a book), I'd say these are the four tips I follow to be true to myself and live that dream life. I split them into handy sections for your reading delight.

Section One: Stop Hitting Yourself. Before you can venture out to find your purpose, you have to truly believe you are worth it. If you don't first believe in yourself enough to try new things, you won't start taking action. My goal is to convince you of the truth that you have incredible potential (I've never met anyone who doesn't), that you can and should love who you are, and that confidence is more about loving your faults than defending your strengths. And that should give you confidence that you too can have confidence. I'm confident about that.

Section Two: Find Your Style. You can't know *your* purpose until you know *your*self. You know yourself only when you pay attention to specific things about yourself. You can know yourself in a way you never have, when you do things in a way you've never done. This section will give you ideas for how to discover things about yourself that will lead to better decision-making when it comes to career, relationships, cheese, and your own happiness.

Section Three: Stop, Collaborate, and Listen. You don't live in isolation, and therefore your identity isn't formed in isolation. Your purpose changes when your environment changes. You will adapt what you just learned in section two by putting your unique spin on the world around you. That's how you figure out both what to do today and what to do to make plans for more long-term, purpose-filled goals for tomorrow.

Section Four: Play Hard, Play Hard. You get excited putting the first three sections into practice, and then life happens. But that moment where it gets hard is where life really changes you for the better, so it's the best time to keep at it. As I always say, "If you're lucky, things won't go according to plan." Things take longer than you wanted, people don't cooperate like you thought, and you get lazy or lose motivation. This section is full of tools to strengthen your mind and your resolve to keep trying at the first three steps. Most importantly, it will remind you that this is your life, and you should enjoy the process. YOLO.

You want to live a life of purpose, because you, your family, your friends, all the humans, and even those puppies will be better off for it. Start with the knowledge that you are already everything you need to be. Then find your style, and adapt the parts of it that fit best with the opportunities you are presented with. If you want to save the world, remember the world is made of people, and a person can't be helped without being listened to. It's not you that changes the world; it's collaboration that changes the world.

Cool. Let's go change the world.

Tip 1:
Stop Hitting Yourself

Stop·Hit·ting·Your·self

/stap 'hɪdɪŋ yɚ'sɜlf/

verb?

1. Often said sarcastically and hypocritically by a sibling who is physically forcing you to hit yourself.
2. An admonition to avoid negative self-talk and believe in your awesomeness and live your best life.

Origin
Probably '80s elementary-school children because they didn't yet have iPads for road trip entertainment.

Example
"The game of slug bug was slow on the long, empty road to Las Vegas, so the older brother satisfied his craving for violence by turning to the younger brother, grabbing his arm, and punching him in the face with it while saying, 'Stop hitting yourself!'"

synonyms: Believe in yourself, Don't put yourself down, You are younger than me, and I am a tyrant.

I'm a pretty confident person, but I wasn't supposed to be.

I was the middle child of seven, which means I got very little attention and was under no illusion that anyone was interested in what I had to say. I lobbied for attention from my parents when it was absolutely essential, like when I saw candy and wanted it, but it wasn't worth all that effort for the small things, so I learned to take care of myself.

I got hurt on our trampoline once, when my brothers bounced me really high and I came down on my wrist. I went inside to tell my mom, but I could see she was busy taking care of my little brother and making us all lunch. I didn't want to add to her plate, so I went on my way. Three days later, when the timing seemed right, I told her my arm was hurting. When she saw how swollen it was, she took me to the doctor, where we found out my wrist was broken. It was honestly one of the best days of my life. I got so much attention that day. And because of my cast, I got a lot of attention from the ladies in my second-grade class. Not too shabby.

It's not that my parents didn't try to give me attention. They did a great job for having seven kids, and I honestly couldn't ask for better parents. It's just that as the middle child, I could very easily see that kids of every age, younger and older, as well as adults, seemed to be just fine whether or not I was around. Basically, no one was asking for my opinion on anything, so I never learned how to have an opinion. This drives my wife nuts because I can never figure out what I want for my birthday. How am I supposed to have an opinion strong enough to tell her how she should spend money on me? In fifth grade, every time someone asked me what I wanted for my birthday, I just said "money." I didn't want to decide. It wasn't greed; it was procrastination.

I still feel like no one really cares about what I have to say. It's an insecurity that makes writing a book like this very tough. Most days I get through a few pages of writing, and then I stand up and yell, "This book is stupid!" Then my wife calms me down.

But if nothing else, the fact that I am *still* writing it (and if you're reading this, I somehow finished it) emphasizes how strongly I feel about how much these things have helped me. I'm thirty years old, and I finally have the courage to form some opinions.

James's opinions (a random sampling):

1. Everyone should try growing their own food. Start with one thing you like. This is really easy if you eat weeds.

2. Everyone has more value and potential than they can use in a lifetime, and therefore everyone can be happy if they choose to be.

3–100. Read the rest of this book.

101. Aliens exist.

You are worth it. It's not a question. It's not about finding out *if* you are worth something, and it's not even about finding out *what* you're worth. It's about recognizing that you have more value and potential than you realize, and that you are so full of that potential that you could be a superstar in every way and still only scratch the surface. If you don't believe me, I hope the chapter on potential will help convince you. Other chapters are about how to unlock that potential and overcome some of the obstacles in the way. Let's do it!

HOW I LEARNED TO LIKE MYSELF

On good days, I know I have something to contribute. I know there is value, deep down inside of me, but the question is, how do I use it? I could be the most valuable person in the world, but if I don't do anything with it, it's still useless.

As I said already, no one needed me to express my opinion as a child. No one appeared to be any better off when I did try to give my two cents. I didn't see the value of my wise and thoughtful thoughts blessing the realms of men. But people seemed to love laughing, and thus, a comedian was born.

I knew I could make people laugh. I wasn't picky—they could be laughing at me or with me. I didn't care. I just knew it felt really good when people laughed. It meant they noticed me. It meant I was giving something to people that made me feel like I was a part of things.

When I was in fourth grade, I had a sleepover with about five friends. That was a huge deal for me, because I didn't have many con-sistent friends. It was one of those situations where I tricked everyone into coming by saying the others were coming, and I crossed that threshold where there were enough people coming that those people decided to actually come. I was hustling for friendship.

That night, all I had to do was pull out the Super Nintendo and the party got started. Other kids were better at coming up with ideas about fun things to do, and I was grateful. One of the kids fell asleep for a moment, so the others found some shaving cream and were getting ready to spray it on his hands and tickle his nose. Classic. But right as they sprayed it in his hands, he woke up. He pushed everyone away and washed his hands off. Everyone was disappointed that their tomfoolery wasn't properly executed, and I was disappointed for them. I could just see how much fun they were about to have, and this fool woke up and ruined it.

I wasn't going to have that. Not at my party. These kids wanted a good laugh and I was going to give it to them.

I gave it a couple hours before I pretended to fall asleep on the couch. I knew it would take a while for them to notice, and to again get the idea to bust out the shaving cream, but I was patient. After almost an hour (Oh, I was committed), they finally noticed me, and the chicanery recommenced. When they sprayed the cream on my hand, I did a little twitch to tease suspense. I made small movements and sounds with my mouth as a true sleeper does. When they tickled my nose, I moved my hand a little, but made them work for it before the big smear. It makes for a better story. I should mention this was only a foreshadowing of what would become a devoted and dignified acting career.

The shaving cream hit my face, and they cheered in victory. I "woke up" to the sound of laughter and played my "realization and disappointment" like a champ. All in all, it was a great party, and I played the long con for one great laugh. It was a success.

And so I used my humor to hide my insecurities, and my insecurities got weaker. I had plenty of weaknesses, but when I was able to see value in myself, I at least had humor as a defense against those weaknesses that kept my insecurities from taking over.

As human beings, we are so insecure. We assume our efforts will be unacceptable unless they are perfect, especially when something important is riding on it. Thinking we have to impress people in order to make money, to get a job, or to do anything we're afraid of not achieving causes a lot of stress.

For example, I was so worried about the title of this book. I came up with over a hundred options, and when I finally found one that my publishers and I all liked, I doubted it and got a knot in my stomach thinking about how nobody would understand what the book was about or care to read it. Meanwhile I was doing research for this book, reading a bunch of books with titles that weren't any more perfect. When I used my paranoid, over-analytical mindset to think about some of those titles, I realized I would have worried about most of them, and yet here I was reading them.

When I look at my real motivation for writing this book, though I may hope for it to help someone, it is mostly to help me. It should be something I'm proud of, as my wife often reminds me. This is the same for my work on Studio C. I can't control who will love it, if it will do good for anyone, or if it will stand the test of time. All I can do is make something that means something to me, that fills a need I have. Otherwise, I'm requiring everyone else's approval before I can have joy and pride in my work. The great thing about solving your own need is that you are also solving it for people with similar needs, and you'll do a better job because you really understand that need. All I can hope for is that this book gives someone the same joy it gives me.

Our insecurity keeps us from truly loving ourselves as we are, failures and all. The good news, and the hard news, is that we are the ones doing it to ourselves. This means we have control, but we are also responsible, which we know is true because of what a real person named Spiderman said about great power. (Note to the pre-Spiderman generation: "With great power comes great responsibility.")

Stop hitting yourself! It's a funny thing we say to our siblings on road trips, but it's also good advice. The way you talk to yourself affects your whole experience in life. This is why I wake up and tell myself I'm beautiful every morning.

We know how important good communication is with others. We need to speak the same language, use body language and tone, and be kind and make sure to listen. The way we speak to others can either lead to a frustrating argument or an uplifting and constructive conversation.

What about communication with ourselves? Are we kind in the way we speak to ourselves? Or do we put ourselves down? Do we use a hopeful, encouraging tone? Or do we say that our mistakes make us hopeless and stupid? Do we speak the same language? Or do we speak French to ourselves, when we can't even understand it? *Je m'appelle un bonbon, voulez-vouz déjà vu la brunette?* These are all important questions.

In later sections of the book, I'll talk about how to *do* what it takes to live your dream life, but none of it will happen until you believe in yourself enough to do it. When things get real, it's what you believe about yourself that will determine if you go forward with confidence or quit with self-pity. So let's get confident.

The good news is you don't actually have to *feel* confident to *be* a confident person. I used to think I had to feel confident in order to do brave things, but that pressure to feel confident actually kept me from doing things I wanted to do. Confidence that actually works is just a belief in yourself, even when you *feel* weird, stupid, and wrong. It's the knowledge that *everyone* feels that way most of the time, and you should never wait for those emotions to go away before you do something. First, those emotions never obey you, and they come and go as they please. Second, the more you wait for them to go away, the stronger they seem to get. It's like standing in quicksand and saying, "I'll wait until I feel free before I attempt to leave." Then you drown in sand.

This is how I discovered the Confidence Triangle, which is a thing I made up. But it works!

THE CONFIDENCE TRIANGLE

Confidence is too often associated with words like "proud," "powerful," and "flawless." These words always have a connotation of being better, having control, and being right as often as possible. The problem with that is that, the majority of the time, you aren't better, you don't have control, and you aren't always right.

The nobler version of confidence is more passive. The words you might use would be "humble," "genuine," and "brave." I love these words, and I think they make a fantastic model for confidence, but I want to take it one step further. Let's redefine these words to make them so usable that you can be confident even on your worst days.

Anyone would be proud to call themselves genuine, brave, and humble. But the reality of those qualities is they require you to be weird, stupid, and wrong, respectively. You can't be genuine without being different, which the haters call weird. You can't be brave unless you do something that your brain tells you is dangerous, which is stupid. You can't be humble unless you embrace being wrong. Imagine how empowered you would be if you loved being weird, stupid, and wrong. It's like how really fit people don't just love being fit, they love being tired, sweaty, and in pain, because they understand that the result is getting fit. (There's a Confidence Triangle version of this too. Gym commercials call it ripped, hydrated, and Chris Pratt.)

THE CONFIDENCE TRIANGLE: WEIRD, STUPID, AND WRONG

Instead of seeing confidence as keeping yourself away from being weird, stupid, and wrong, see it as embracing these traits, and then truly nothing can get you down.

Someone calls you weird because you love to paint cheese. "Yay! I'm genuine, and I contribute something completely unique to the world, instead of the same thing everyone thinks they need to contribute. Happy to be called weird." I really do love cheese, as evident in the following painting.

You really want to learn the saxophone, but it costs ten times more than any other instrument. "Yay! I'm brave, because it's better to spend ten dollars on something that truly makes me happy than to pay one dollar for something that adds nothing to my life. Happy to be called stupid."

You give someone a gift of nice shoes, but they are offended because they are a mermaid. "Yay! I'm humble, because even if my intentions are good, I can still be inconsiderate. What a lesson to learn! Happy to be called wrong."

Confident does not mean outgoing or loud. It doesn't mean you never doubt yourself; in fact, confident people have the confidence to doubt themselves without getting down on themselves about it. Because that's what confidence really is: the ability to take whatever comes to you and know that you are okay. It's knowing that you have power over your life, over the things that really matter. It's accepting that you may not always be able to change your environment, but you can always change your response to it. You are worth it (as affirmed by the L'Oreal ads). You are comfortable with your-self when you are being genuine. When you are pretending, you are not comfortable.

I'll come back to these a lot in this book, because I'm weird, stupid, and wrong. If you ever think you're lonely in feeling that way, you're not. In fact, I want to convince you that feeling this way is a sure sign that you're doing things right.

To be clear, you don't need to seek out ways to be weird, stupid, or wrong. You can make a lot of poor choices when your *goal* is to be weird, stupid, or wrong. This is the Confidence Triangle, not the YOLO Triangle. In the next chapter, we'll talk about how you can base your choices on discovering yourself and being genuinely you. But we need the Confidence Triangle first, because even if you are true to yourself, you will run into situations where you are weird, stupid, and wrong, and I don't want it to stop you.

You can love yourself before you even know yourself, just like anyone else you love—always getting to know them, and accepting change as they grow. People we know and love still surprise us, and

Here is a recent picture of me being weird, stupid, and wrong.

that can be true of our relationships with ourselves too. And then you can surprise yourself, like, "Oh, hey there, me. Good job on those drums. I didn't realize I had so much rhythm. What a special little surprise."

The more comfortable you are with yourself, the more willing you are to do uncomfortable things, and it's the uncomfortable things that create growth.

So how do you become comfortable with yourself?

MY DEFINITION OF GENUINE

First, be genuine. I believe that everyone is *inherently* good but *naturally* bad. Your soul, your spirit, your personality, or whatever you want to call it, is always inherently good. But without effort, you will succumb to your carnal nature, be lazy, selfish, impatient, and all that. Your body and brain are tools, and they need to be maintained on purpose in order for them to perform properly.

So when I say genuine, I don't mean just being you. I mean being your best self, the person you want to be, and the person that you would be if you were able to live up to your potential. Just because you feel like doing something in the moment doesn't mean it is genuine. It is not genuine to give up on something you love because you feel like giving up; you are acting out of laziness. It is not genuine to be mean to someone because they wronged you; you are acting out of anger.

Let me put it this way. If everyone were genuine, we would have world peace. While people would still *feel* the frustration, anger, laziness, and fear that come with life, they would never *act* on those negative feelings. They would choose instead to overcome their carnal nature and act according to the good in them. If you are being genuine, you are being the incredible person that you are. I'm not saying the incredible person that you *could* be. You are already a really good person, but if you don't like the way you act, maybe you need to practice being genuine.

Jesus was genuine. He laughed, He cried, and He got upset, just like anyone else. But He was always genuine, even in the face of death.

25

He believed in service and He always served. He believed in His divine calling even though many people hated Him for it. You will be hated for doing what you believe in, but that isn't the reason you are doing it. Jesus did what He did because it was the right thing for Him to do, and billions of followers are grateful to Him for it.

He's certainly not the only spiritual leader to feel this way. Buddha believed our pure self was the best self. He said, "If with a pure mind a person speaks or acts, happiness follows them like a never-departing shadow." Not a bad way to live. Just the word "pure" itself means we haven't added anything. There is no good that needs to be added to you; you are the good.

Gandhi said, "Be congruent, be authentic, be your true self." And if you feel like you need to find some impressive-sounding purpose, remember what Gandhi, who did a ton of good, said about his purpose, "My life is my message." Boom.

I always try to be genuine just for the sake of my sanity. If you try to be what other people want you to be, you'll never satisfy anyone, especially yourself.

If you are a fan of Studio C and you happened to meet me, you could easily be disappointed. Depending on my mood, I might be really quiet and just nod, or I'd want to chat too much when you would rather get a picture and never talk to me again. People are sometimes disappointed because instead of wanting to know me, they want me to meet their expectations. Sometimes they even want me to perform for them, like in the middle of the grocery store, which is awkward. The best person to recognize me in public is someone who just barely knows who I am, either from Studio C or, of course, this best-selling book. Like, they wouldn't stop me if I was walking by, but if they're in line with me anyway, and I almost make eye contact with them, they strike up a conversation. They would say something like, "Hey, I've consumed a fair portion of your work, and I appreciate it." (Or "I hate it.") And I would say, "Thank you!" (Or "That makes sense.")

Basically, I like being a normal human being. We all like to be ourselves and be treated with respect as ourselves. By the way, it's not lost on me that it is a really cool thing that I can be just walking down the street and, every once in a while, someone will yell out, "You're awesome!" to which I respond, "No, you're awesome!" And it's a good time.

Be genuine and let others be genuine. No one is perfect at it, so let's just be kind to each other.

UNLOCK YOUR POTENTIAL

I'm a big believer in potential. I also believe we don't use nearly as much of our potential as we could.

Think about the sun for moment. We know it's massive beyond our ability to grasp, and we know it's really hot. All it does all day—and all it has done all day for billions of years, by the way—is burn things up. And Earth only gets a tiny fraction of that energy, about one billionth.

Yet everything on Earth is made from the sun. The sun gives heat to the water and energy to the plants, and the animals eat the plants, and we eat the animals and the plants. Nothing would be here without the sun, and yet there is enough energy being wasted by the sun to power a billion earths.

On top of that, the tiny fraction of sun we do get could power all the electricity in the world many times over, if only we could harness that potential. In fact, according to the Land Art Generator Initiative, all it would take to provide plenty of power to the entire world is enough solar panels to cover Spain, which is tiny compared to the whole Earth.[1] So, Spain, stop being so selfish.

When you put it that way, it seems insane that we wouldn't put all our effort into creating enough solar panels to have completely renewable energy.

That's how I want you to feel about yourself.

When you know your potential, you will suddenly feel like it would be insane not to harness that potential. For better or worse, this is why "Get Rich Quick" books hook you. They are trying to imitate your ability to tap into your potential. The problem with those books and seminars and pyramid schemes is that they often aren't based on your reality. They dazzle you with the result of hard work, without telling you it actually takes hard work. Or worse, they dazzle you with promises that can never be fulfilled, because their system isn't real, and they know it.

So welcome to my "Get Rich Quick" scheme, where you probably won't get rich and it isn't actually quick.

It's more like the sun: a slow burn. In fact, unlike a human being, the sun only has one talent. But even if your only talent is burning things, if you do it well, and you keep at it, slowly but surely you will be the cause of every beautiful thing created in your world. Or you'll be a pyromaniac.

Most of us have many talents, and you might focus on one or the other at different points in your life, but there is one thing that you have that is absolute. It's going to sound really cheesy. Are you ready for it?

Your absolute talent is *yourself.*

Cute, right?

My friend Natalie has a poster at her desk that I love. It says, "No one is you. That is your power."

But what does that really mean? Well, that's kind of the point of the rest of this book. It means that when you know yourself and you are true to yourself, you will make the best choices, you will do your best work, and you will feel so blessed that you want to bless the whole world, and you'll do it in ways no one else can.

Speaking of "Get Rich Quick," when I was in college, I tried summer sales. It was miserable. If you're not familiar with summer sales, consider yourself lucky. First, I tried doing pest control, walking door to door, impressing people with my big chemical words. I tried to scare people into paying way too much for pest control, and I tried even harder to act like I cared about what I was saying.

That first attempt only lasted two weeks until I quit. The next summer rolled around and the lure of making a lot of money over the summer had me considering it again. This time, though, the recruit-ment meeting was held at the Brick Oven restaurant, so I got free pizza when I went. I went three times so I could "ask questions."

This time was also different because it wasn't pest control; it was something I actually believed in. It was a company called Living Scriptures. They make animated stories from the scriptures so you can learn the stories in a more fun way. I grew up watching these things, and the scripture stories I know the best are the ones that I could hear and visualize in my mind from those movies.

So, I was ready to go out and make my first million that summer, and I was sure to succeed because I believed in the product. How could I not sell to everyone with ears and a propensity for religious education?

It was miserable. No matter how much I appreciated this product, I couldn't promise anyone that they *needed* it and it would *guarantee* them a better life. It's not like they *couldn't* learn the scriptures with-out them. I was also just miserable talking about the same thing day in and day out, trying to convince other people to spend their money. I'm personally a scrooge when it comes to money, so it was very insincere for me to act like I thought it was wise to "sign up immediately or lose this great deal."

That time I made it six weeks until I quit.

Cut to about eight years later. I'd been working on Studio C and gaining traction as a public figure. Living Scriptures was interested in using a personality from Studio C in a commercial. I was interested! I did a commercial for them, and it was a great experience. They liked working with me, and they asked if I would be interested in being a spokesperson for the company. I was interested!

Now I have this gig where I am once again selling Living Scriptures movies, but in a way that I really enjoy. I was so miserable selling Living Scriptures during that summer, but the problem was the way I was doing it. And since I was miserable, I never got very good at it. Doing it in a way that I love, and having fun while I'm doing it, has made me better at it. At the time of writing this, I'm still a spokesper-son for them, and we're coming up with new and better ideas all the time. I always had the potential to sell Living Scriptures, but I couldn't do it well until I did it sincerely.

It makes me wonder what potential I have that I'm not harnessing. What potential do you have that you aren't harnessing? I believe you have more than you'll ever be able to use. Instead of worrying about who likes you, think instead about how many meaningful friendships you could have if you took the time to *be* a good friend to others? There's no limit. What skills or interests could you discover if you took only ten extra minutes a day to try something new? That's only ten fewer minutes of playing Fortnite or doing your makeup or watching ice cream melt.

Don't settle for less. If you would rather have anyone's life other than your own, your perspective needs work. Kurt Cobain said, "Wanting to be someone else is a waste of the person you are."[2] You need to believe more in your potential, because you would be surprised what you can make out of the sourest lemons. Hint: It's lemonade.

Not believing in your potential is like having a gold mine in your backyard, but you decide to dig through your junk drawer and hold a garage sale to get some cash. Yeah, it takes some work to dig it out, *but it's gold!*

(When my wife helped me edit this book, it was very important to her that I acknowledge how people refer to boogers as gold nuggets, and picking your nose as digging for gold. Thank you very much, Brenna, for your contribution. It has not been in vain.)

You know it would be ridiculous not to dig up that gold. It doesn't matter how lazy you are; it would be worth it. In fact, the main reason people are lazy is because they don't actually believe they have a gold mine in their backyard. Well, now you know, because I just told you.

Disclaimer: this is an analogy for your personal potential. I am not liable if you do not have an actual gold mine in your backyard. I am not responsible for any negative consequences associated with or costs you may incur digging holes in your backyard. However, if you are on your butt or on your phone too much, you should probably go outside and dig holes. Maybe plant something in that hole. Or just fill

Life Lemonade

1. Lemons
2. Happy Songs
3. Teddy Bears
4. Optimism

TAKE ALL THE INGREDIENTS AND
MIX THEM WITH A HUG MACHINE.
DON'T PUT ICE IN IT, BECAUSE IT
WILL JUST MELT FROM THE HUGS.

ENJOY IMMEDIATELY!

it up again for a little exercise. Or just have a hole there, and it will remind you of this analogy. I'm done talking about digging holes.

But why do we not know this already? If we have all this potential, why haven't we heard about it? Why do we assume all there is is what we can see on the surface? We all know the media doesn't help. We've heard about their negative messages so many times we could list them off in our sleep (after falling asleep with the TV on). Why do they do that? Are they evil? No, it's because they are selling what's on the surface. There is nothing inherently wrong with material things; we need them to live. The problem comes when we start to subconsciously believe that they are the *only* things we need, because we spend so much time watching these messages, AKA letting people tell us how important material things are.

But it's even deeper than that. It's not just material things that distract us. Entitlement, laziness, complacency—these are all just symptoms of one big failure: not knowing ourselves. The more you know yourself, the more you can realize your potential. When you see the good you produce, your confidence builds and builds, and soon enough nothing can stop you from being a powerful source of good. The energy you get from this will be so satisfying that it will be your only desire. It works better than caffeine!

Every choice you make, whether toward or away from living your potential, will affect the *power* you have to use that potential. That power is earned. When NASA sends a rocket to space, it takes so much study and work from thousands of people to get everything working right to do something great. The laws of physics and chemistry must be understood and followed. If we understand the laws of the self just as well, digging in and figuring it out, putting in that much time and work, we gain a power most people only dream of. Great people (athletes, inventors, professors, etc.) often have teams of people surrounding them to bring the greatness out of them. The potential in one person is so great. The potential of a united team is even greater.

I have an app on my phone that automatically sends me a daily quote. They are all super inspiring, but they do very little for me. Why wouldn't inspirational quotes inspire me? Because quotes don't change people. The power to change lies in the work it takes to make change. Reading one quote won't do that. If you have context for a quote, it can serve as a quick reminder of what you already know, but hearing it once on its own probably won't have a lasting effect. You just can't get around putting in the work to bring out your potential.

So now that I've bashed the idea of quotes, I'd like to share a quote. "Knowledge is of no value unless you put it into practice," said Anton Chekhov. If you don't apply your knowledge, it will have no connection to reality. I love the following image that expresses this idea in a cool way.

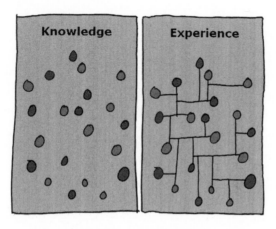

Originally drawn by cartoonist Hugh MacLeod

Even a simple change of your body language can bring out some of your potential. The act of smiling can make you happy. Amy Cuddy, a social psychologist, showed that putting people in positions of power actually changes the chemistry of their body to match those in power.[3] They would suddenly have higher testosterone and lower cortisol (the stress hormone), causing them to physically feel more empowered. Just standing in a powerful position for two minutes, with your hands on your hips, significantly changes your body chemistry.

Body language is even powerful enough to change other people. Nalani Ambady, a researcher at Tufts University, had people watch 30-second soundless clips of physician-patient interactions and had them judge the physician's niceness.[4] Keep in mind, they were just watching them without hearing anything. Here's the crazy part. Their judgments accurately predicted whether the physician would be sued or not. What?! Doctors are more likely to get sued if they just *seem* less nice by their body language? Subjects also ranked the doctors' competence, but that had no correlation to their likeliness of getting sued. It was all in the body language. That doctor never would have been sued if he had just resisted the urge to Nae Nae. That's so 2015.

Albert Einstein talked about the "optical delusion of everyday consciousness," which basically means that we only think something is real if we can understand it. This delusion is what keeps us from living up to our potential, because we require proof that something works *before* we actually try it.

Consider the consciousness of societies one thousand years ago, or even just one hundred years ago. It used to be "truth" that if you went over 15 mph, you would die. It used to be "truth" that bacteria don't exist, and the sickness is evil blood inside you, and you had to get rid of your blood. If you died (probably from loss of blood), you were just too evil to be cured. It used to be "truth" less than one hundred years ago that you can't send a picture to someone invisibly through the sky, but now we can do that within seconds through texting.

One of my favorite stupid quotes is from Charles H. Duell, who is known for only one thing, which is the quote, "Everything that can be invented has been invented." He said this in 1899.

It's not that they could ever prove these things were impossible; they just had no idea how they could be. Without proof we doubt; without explanation we dismiss. I think one of the biggest reasons we are improving technology so fast is not just because we are "on a roll," but simply because we believe we can. Ancient civilizations had advanced technologies that have been discovered all over the world, but they didn't advance their technology as quickly. In Baghdad, archaeologists found batteries dating back to about 200 BC. They were made with clay pots and copper discs. So why didn't they invent the iPhone? Even though Baghdadi inventor Smeve Snobs had the idea, everyone said it would be ridiculous to carry around all those pot batteries. Instead of figuring out a way to make it smaller, he gave up on his dream. If only he had read my incredible book, he might have believed it was still worth it to try, and we would have flying cars and cheeseburger printers by now.

Just because you can't prove something is possible doesn't mean it isn't. Just because you can't prove you have infinite potential doesn't mean you don't.

Are you worried that your contribution doesn't matter? Don't be. Mother Theresa is, by all accounts, a great hero of our time. She is someone who used her potential to do incredible things. Still she said, "What we are doing is nothing more than a drop in the ocean." If Mother Theresa can feel that her contribution was small, it makes total sense that we feel that way. That shouldn't deter you from doing it. She continues by saying, "But if the drop were not there, the ocean would be missing something."

As the wise emperor says in the Disney classic *Mulan*, "A single grain of rice can tip the scale."[5]

We all feel small in our efforts, but that's the way it is for every great person who has ever lived. This book is about finding what couple of things we can do. You *can* be Mother Theresa in one area. You *should* be Martin Luther King Jr. in one area, or Gandhi or Beyoncé or the kid who said "apparently" on a newscast so many times that Ellen fell in love with him and has had him on her show multiple times. Your thing doesn't need to be public, because publicity and fame are not the point. Maybe I could be the Mother Theresa of comedic engineers, going around bringing joy and laughter to nerds at local comic cons throughout the western United States. I may not have changed the world, but I made *their* world better for an hour or two.

Every once in a while, you see people doing great things get featured on the news. Some old guy finally gets recognition for the sacrifices he made over sixty years of being a schoolteacher. These people don't seem to care that they've spent their lives doing something great and only get recognized by a news station for a few minutes. They aren't doing it for the recognition, or for anything other reason than being genuine, because when you are genuine, you are happy.

Because you have consciousness and choice, you can define the shape of the world by your choices. Your mind and mood are completely subject to your thoughts. Your words have the power to influence the people around you. Your actions set the future in motion. You are not a lone being trying to survive; you are the sun with a choice of whether you will fill the world with light or just burn out inside yourself.

WHY SO SERIOUS?

Now that you know you have all this potential, you might be tempted to take yourself too seriously. The best way I've found to destroy my creativity and stress myself out is to take myself too seriously.

The first two times I tried out for Divine Comedy at BYU, taking it too seriously might have been the actual reason I didn't make it in. It might seem counterintuitive to take comedy seriously, but I really wanted it, and when we want something badly (comedy or not) we can take it too seriously because of our fear of failure.

I was so worried about impressing people that I forgot to have fun. I was competitive and ambitious, and the cast wasn't looking for a competitive, self-indulgent person to join them. On my third time auditioning, I wasn't even thinking of getting in. I just thought the audition was fun, and I maintained that attitude throughout the callbacks. To my pleasant surprise, I got the call that afternoon, and I had no idea my life would forever be changed. And it never would have happened if I had again taken myself too seriously.

So why do we do it? We think something has to be a certain way, so we stress out about it. "I have to get in to this fun group, so I need to step over everyone who is having fun to get in!" If it doesn't go our way, we assume something terrible will happen. Things that we deem "important" need to be done right, because they are too important for us to fail.

It's understandable, because what's the alternative? Do we just go around not caring about what happens? Are we supposed to be complacent and let anything happen, with no resistance and no fighting for what we think is right? That doesn't seem right either. So, this is the best way I've come up with to still work hard for what you want, yet never frustrate yourself with stress and worry: see life as a game!

People work hard to win games. I haven't seen my Studio C friends work harder than they do when they play Smash Brothers. They are intense. I am terrible at video games, so my best defense is to pick a character that is good at avoiding everyone else while they beat each other. Then out of the eight people playing, I can sometimes get in the top three and pretend I did something to earn it. I have to work extra hard, but one time it paid off. We were playing Halo, and by some miracle I was the last man standing. I jumped up from my chair and shouted, "I won Nintendo!" and then immediately went home. I quit while I was ahead so I could leave with my pride intact. That pride was immediately destroyed the next night, but whatever.

See life as a game, and even if you are terrible at it, you can take pride in your little victories. It helps to go home and do a puzzle for six-year-olds, then look at your nine-month-old daughter who can't do that puzzle and say, "Looks like I know some things after all."

Look at the best athletes. They work harder than most people, and all they are doing is getting better at playing a game. If they miss a shot or a hit or a splat or whatever it is in their respective sport, they try not to stress about it. They just keep going, enjoying the challenge, and being the best at what they do just because they want to be good at it.

Imagine if life was like that. Instead of freaking out every time you have to take a test, see it as a fun challenge. You're perfectly willing to learn the rules of a game. How is that different than learning the rules of math? The only difference is you assign some great importance to it.

But James, my math test is more important than a game. If I fail school, I will die. There's no getting around that.

The truth is, you will not do any better by stressing about it, and studies show you will likely do better if you have fun with it. In the book *Einstein Never Used Flashcards* by Kathy Hirsh-Pasek and Roberta Michnick Golinkoff, they talk about how some kids are put into school too early. Instead of learning by playing, which is how humans naturally learn, they are forced at a young age to memorize flash cards and math tables. What was the result? The kids didn't do any better in school than kids who started in kindergarten. In fact, they were more stressed out about school and later did worse, because they were conditioned to think school was irrelevant to actual experience.

The older we get, the better we get at creating context for what we learn. So no, I'm not giving you an excuse to stop doing your homework and quit school so you can attempt to create a multimillion-dollar lemonade stand empire. I'm glad I finished school instead of following through with that plan.

I'm just saying you should be more of a snowboard announcer and less of a figure skating announcer. I was watching the winter Olympics recently and I was surprised by what some of the judges were saying. You have these figure skaters that are killing themselves, day in and day out, to become the best in the world. And they have! They're at the Olympics! Yet one of the skaters did a triple spin thing instead of a quadruple spin thing and the announcers literally called her "disgraceful." Just to drive it home, some synonyms for "disgraceful" are *shameful*, *contemptible*, *offensive*, and *opprobrious*. And I would *never* call an athlete of that stature opprobrious. I would probably never call anyone opprobrious because I'm not convinced that's really a word and I think the thesaurus is pranking me.

The snowboarder announcers, on the other hand: "Whoa! That guy was fast," and "That guy was fast too," and the ever-observant "Look at how fast she's going!" These announcers were having the time of their lives. The snowboarders were having the time of their lives. They were all hugging each other and sincerely cheering for each other. That's the life I like to live, and that's what this chapter is about.

If you're anything like me, you're probably thinking, *Come on, James. Surely there are some things in life we should take seriously. Are you really saying we should never take anything seriously? Don't be ridiculous,*

James. Because also if you're anything like me, you have multiple personalities that argue with each other.

I like to go back to the basics. Why do you feel the need to take it seriously? What do you have to lose that is so important?

To understand my perspective, I think it's important to understand what I believe about life, namely that everything will be okay. How do I know that? Because you'll always have what you need. Because you don't actually need anything that you can't control. Because you only *think* you need things, because you *want* what those things give you.

For example, you think you need a specific job. You only need that job because you want money. You only need money because you want to buy food. You only need food because you want to live. The worst-case scenario is death, and either heaven is real or you have no soul and you won't know the difference. That is a very, very basic way to explain that you don't actually need anything outside of yourself.

So, by all means, if it genuinely matters to you, take the thing seriously! But only in a temporary way, without the need to get a certain result.

You can take games seriously. People get very invested in games, emotionally and physically. It's an amazing feeling to be a part of a team and not let people down. Loyalty to others is a great thing to be taken seriously.

But what happens when you fail at a game? You keep playing. If you're caught up in it, you might be frustrated for a minute, but mostly you just keep shooting, or swinging, or throwing, or bouncing (according to your respective sport).

It's called being a good sport. And if you can learn to be a good sport about life, it's a paradigm shift that empowers you to face every challenge that comes your way with bravery and energy.

To be totally honest, a lot of people aren't even that great at doing this *while* they play a game. They forget that the whole point was to have fun challenging yourself. Not only do they take life too seriously, but they also take playing games too seriously, and then they hit me when I score a goal for the other team. Hey! I still made *a* goal!

This happened when I was about twelve. I scored a goal for the wrong side when I was playing soccer, or maybe basketball. I failed at too many sports to remember which one I happened to be playing during this particular sports failure. But I remember running up to my dad excitedly. Just to give you an idea of how often I scored a goal, my parents told me that if I ever scored they would take the whole family out to a pizza dinner. No pressure, just another way to fail my siblings who were already forced to come to my games. But at least it gave them a reason to watch.

At this particular game (it must have been soccer now that I think about it), I had scored a goal. I'd had a few zero-point games behind me, so this victory was particularly sweet. Of course, when I told my Dad which pizza place I wanted to eat at, he explained that it didn't count, because I scored for the other team.

I'm sorry, did I not kick a soccer ball (maybe it actually was basketball . . .) into a goal? Is that not just as impressive regardless of which side of the court (nah, I swear it was a soccer field) the goal happened to be on? Same size goal, same ball, same me. Dad wouldn't budge.

From my perspective, if the rules of the goal-for-pizza promise were not going to be respected *as stated*, then I had no further interest in sports. I had reached my full potential in that arena, and I needed not waste any more time on it. So, I quit and never played hockey again.

This is why I see life as a game. Because if anything is so important that your mistakes can ruin it and therefore ruin your life, you have little hope as an imperfect human being. We know there is no reason to be insecure when we play video games, yet there have been cases where someone did make a video game too important. There may have been a person, who will not be named, who got so frustrated he threw the controller at the TV and broke the volume button. I won't say who it was, but his name starts with *J* and ends with *ames Perry*. When my dad found out, he was pretty upset . . . at whoever that was.

If we can take a game and make it too important, then who's to say we don't take life and make it too important? You might be taking some things too seriously.

Here's what's great about this perspective. We can see obstacles in life as a challenge rather than a nuisance. If we used to wish for a life without obstacles, we now welcome them with open arms. Without obstacles, life would be a long, boring road to death. We live, we glide, we die. Now, it's time to change the word *obstacle* to *challenge*! Ooh, what a fun word!

We can completely change the way we look at the obstacles in front of us. When I'm trying to get something done, and something else seems to be in my way, I can decide to be upset and frustrated with it, or I can decide to say "bring it on" and make it a fun challenge. Here's a simple example. So simple it happened while I was writing this.

I was taking care of my four-month-old daughter, June, in the morning, while my wife was in the other room resting. June didn't want anything other than to be held. I was starving, and I didn't want to wait until my wife was up in order to eat, but I couldn't put my baby down or else she would start complaining about life (she hasn't read this book yet). In that moment I decided to apply the principle of seeing it as a challenge. And I thought, "Bring it on! Let's see what I can do with the baby in one hand." So, I put her in my left hand and I was flying around the kitchen, showing off my skills, skills that I discovered as I performed them (an added measure of fun and discovery), and made a morning of it. I opened the bread with one hand to get a couple pieces in the toaster. I got the jam and butter out of the fridge. I buttered and jammed my bread, poured my drink, and had a great time showing off to my little girl all the things I can do with one hand. I was so excited I went in the other room, got my phone, and wrote this section of the book with one hand. I did have to use dictation, so if Siri misunderstood anything I said, there will be some hairs. Errors End of sentence Period Never mind and dictation and dictation know and dictation note EMD end. Like the end of the world. Thank you.

41

How can you ever know what you're made of if you are never challenged to do things you've never done? You may think it's a silly thing to discover that you can make breakfast with one hand while keeping a baby happy and safe (I quickly realized keeping her safe was part of the deal. Not that I bumped her head. I didn't bump her head. Stop thinking I bumped her head! Dang it, my wife is going to read this.), but it's not all that silly. It was at least as fun as winning a video game. I actually thought it was more fun, but I guess I'm just the domestic type.

This is how you slowly dig up all that gold we talked about in the chapter on potential. Not all the gold you find will be large nuggets, but they will still be gold. I promise you they will feel like gold, and they are worth just as much per ounce as any nuggets you find. More importantly, you can't find the nuggets without the pleasures of a few small flakes. But isn't that a beautiful thing? It's not a wasteland of dirt along the way, just smaller versions of joy on your way to the big ones. But I admit, when you find the big nuggets of gold, it is pretty dang amazing.

(Yes, Brenna, it is very funny to think of the entire previous paragraph in terms of boogers. Thank you for pointing that out again in your edit.)

THE ONLY THING TO FEAR IS ~~FEAR ITSELF~~ QUICKSAND

We all have someone we turn to when we need help. I have a friend who I would always turn to when I was afraid of the future, of my failures, or of all the meanies in the world. Here is a conversation we had:

Me: I don't know if my friends really like me.

Friend: You are pretty weird, and you tend to get annoying, so calm down and stop talking or people might stop hanging out with you.

Me: Oh. Okay.

Friend: I don't think they miss you when you're gone. Also, if you don't show up, they're probably talking behind your back.

Me: Tough to hear, but I'll keep that in mind. Also, I feel kind of lost, emotionally and spiritually.

Friend: What have you done that made God mad at you? You need to fix that or be punished. I hope you can, but you might be one of those people who just can't deal with life. You might just be a sad person.

Me: Hurtful. Okay. I'll be sure to let that haunt my dreams. Can I ask you for one more bit of advice?

Friend: You're a really needy person, but sure.

Me: *starts to tear up* Um, I'm not sure how to choose the right career.

Friend: I only know one thing. You will ruin your life if you do anything other than work constantly at figuring this out until you get it right. At that point, you can enjoy life, but until then any fun you have will be a huge waste of time and put you behind. I just hope you didn't already miss the boat. I don't know how you'll ever catch up to Rick "The Wonder Kid" Smithers.

Me: *Curls up in a ball and weeps*

END SCENE

Isn't it great to have a friend who's honest? Does this friend maybe seem a little too brutal? Hostile even?

This friend was . . . *me*!

Did I just blow your mind??? No? K.

Ever heard the saying "we are our own worst critics"? We come up with a lot of ways to justify our fears and blame ourselves for everything that has gone wrong or can go wrong. But we aren't to blame for what happens to us; we are only responsible for *our response* to it. If we respond poorly, we become miserable. If we respond well, we become joyful. It's great that it's totally up to us, but with great power comes great responsibility, and fear is a stubborn little punk.

Fear is natural. It is primal, and it is meant to help us come up with worst-case scenarios so we are prepared for danger. The earliest humans were preparing to not get mauled by mountain lions. Today, we are preparing to not lose followers on Instagram. It's a dangerous world out there.

Fear stops being helpful when we start assigning blame. You should definitely have fear about jumping off of a cliff, but that doesn't mean you should blame yourself for not being able to land the fall. It's ridiculous to think anyone would do that, but we basically do that every time we blame ourselves for our circumstances. Even if you could land it, you would still get down on yourself for not being able to land it as nicely as Rick. Boo, Rick! Show off.

We do this for the future as well. The reason you chicken out of asking a girl on a date is not because you think she will physically harm you, but because when she inevitably rejects you, you know you will blame yourself. You don't speak up to your boss, because if she reacts poorly to it, you will blame yourself for her reaction. Just because you triggered that reaction does not mean you are responsible for it.

Have you ever heard of the butterfly effect? To sum up, every action has the potential to drastically change the future. Even the flap of a butterfly's wings can cause a slight change in wind, causing a seed to be blown in a slightly different direction, causing a plant to grow, and that plant happens to be a serial killer plant, and it murders everyone, and so on. You get the picture.

This means two great things. First, it isn't your fault if your boss reacts poorly, because all the butterflies are equally to blame for the events leading up to that reaction. Your action just happens to be the most recent. Second, there are infinite things changing the future at any given moment, so you are not responsible for controlling the future. It may be scary that the future isn't totally in your control, but the truth is, if it were, you would mess it up. So, it would actually be scarier if you completely controlled the future.

44

Take control of your life by relinquishing control of your life. Sounds counterintuitive, I know. But you're really just relinquishing the *perception* of control over something that you have absolutely zero control over. You can control yourself, your actions, and your thoughts, and those are the only things that make the difference between happiness and misery. Don't fear what will happen to you in the future. Let it be tough, let it be painful, and let it be glorious.

In high school, while I was telling myself how my friends didn't like me or respect me very much, my real friends showed me otherwise. I went to a sleepover, and I arrived a bit late. Most of them were already there and having fun. We had a rule in my family, inspired by our religious beliefs, that we didn't watch rated-R movies, and my friends knew about it. It was one of the many things that made me different, which of course was a source of pride at times and a source of loneliness at other times. When I showed up to the party, they were watching a rated-R movie and enjoying it. I could hear them laughing as I walked in. Before I even knew what was going on, one of them said, "Guys, James is here. Turn it off." I didn't understand yet why he was saying it, so my first reaction was to feel like I was being mocked or left out intentionally. But it was followed by, "Yeah, we don't watch rated-R movies when James is here. Let's do something else."

None of them had religious convictions about rated-R movies; they just had love and respect for me. I still felt a little self-conscious making everyone stop their movie (blaming myself), but they assured me that they didn't want to watch it. Throughout high school they did little things like that to show me they respected me and loved me for being true to myself.

Keep in mind, this wasn't the case with all my friends. I had other friends who never really got it, never cared about my beliefs, and honestly might have thought less of me for it. But that's okay. It turns out, whether you live genuinely or not, some people will like you and some people won't. The only difference is that *you* will like you when you're genuine.

You may have the same self-doubt everyone has, but you will gain the confidence to be happy with yourself deep down. Remember, the Confidence Triangle requires that we be weird, so if they think you're weird, yay! You did it!

The author Isaac Lidsky said, "Fear replaces the unknown with the awful."[6] The future is unknown, and if we give into fear, we often see fear's prophesies fulfilled. Lidsky started going blind at age twelve as his retinas slowly deteriorated until age twenty-five, when everything went dark. In his TED Talk, "What Reality Are You Creating For Yourself?" he said, "I knew blindness would ruin my life. . . . It was the end of achievement for me. . . . I knew it. . . . It was a lie, but it was my reality." He talked about how we create our realities, and that he had to decide that his blindness was not a curse before he could be truly happy. "For me, going blind was a profound blessing, because my blindness gave me vision."[7]

Helen Keller, who was both blind and deaf, said something similar: "The only thing worse than being blind is having sight but no vision."

Get vision! That's the point. That's the reason to find yourself, which is the next section of this book. This book is about gaining vision. It's about learning who you are and what hopes for the future you can dig up as you bravely explore the world around you. And you won't bravely explore if you keep giving in to your fear.

Courage is how you fight through fear. "Courage is not the absence of fear, but the awareness that something else is more important." Either Stephen R. Covey or Franklin D. Roosevelt said that. Maybe both. I couldn't figure it out, which is weird, because everything on the internet is completely credible and accurate. Courage works great when you can't get rid of your fear, *but* there is also a way to get rid of fear, and that is love.

The opposite of fear is love. Going back to my amazing fear example, the possible rejection of the girl would not be an issue if you were doing it out of love. If you cared only for her, you would not fear any rejection or loss, because you wouldn't be doing it for selfish reasons.

In summary, you will get the best result if you approach people with love, whether or not you get the result you expected. Your love for them and yourself will overcome your fear. Jesus Christ taught something very powerful when he said, "Perfect love casteth out all fear." That's what I believe too.

Now, go pump yourself up by hopping on to YouTube and listening to "The Power of Love" by Huey Lewis while you make some popcorn for the next chapter.

TREAT YO SELF! WITH RESPECT

In sixth grade, I took what I knew about how to make people laugh, and I ventured into the realm of pain comedy. It's like physical comedy, except it hurts.

I would jump off the swings and dive into the ground. I would actually swing as high as I could, jump off, lean forward, and dive into the bark. Matt Meese would have loved it. There is nothing funnier to that man than a solid, well-timed smack to the face. Jason obliges pretty often, writing sketches that require real pain for him. My swing diving probably looked funny, and people laughed, but I think it was a low point in my comedy career in terms of self-respect.

It wasn't genuine, because I wasn't respecting myself, and in the end it didn't get a good result. That is what always happens when you sacrifice your self-respect to try to please other people. You might not even really please anyone, and even if you do please them momentarily, it doesn't last. People are actually turned off by self-disrespect. If they seem to want it, it's really just a façade, because it only results in them pitying you or feeling like they are better than you or can take advantage of you. Your value in their eyes gets lowered to the value you are portraying, instead of your real value.

The nose-diving, hair-tussling, get-up-with-pieces-of-bark-stuck-in-my-face bit didn't last long. It got fewer laughs every time I did it.

So, where could I go from there? I had to either revitalize the bit and maybe throw in a broken collarbone, or find a new way to relate to people, like, I don't know, a normal hobby or something. Go big or go home. I'm happy to say I chose the latter.

When you believe in your potential and you start to build your confidence, you realize you don't need to sacrifice your self-respect for anything. You don't need to pretend to be anything other than who you are, and you don't need to do anything you aren't comfortable with. Easier said than done, right?

In middle school, the result of all my self-disrespect was that I didn't really maintain any close friendships. I basically had to start over. I was lucky to have a loving family, and my brother Greg was my closest brother, but he was also fourteen and distracted by his own middle school nightmare.

I also had just spent a week at my friend's place while my parents were out of town. He would never admit it, and I shouldn't either, but we spent maybe two hours in his room lip-syncing *NSYNC to each other. If that's not a bonding moment, I don't

Most Halloweens of my childhood, I dressed up as a color, as you can clearly see in this black-and-white photo. Here is Greg, dressed up as a clown, or "a middle school nightmare."

know what is. Except it didn't bond us. It was the last thing we ever did as friends. I showed up on the first day of school and he pretended like he didn't know me. But he did know me. He knew the *NSYNC side of me, and he acted like it meant nothing! Anyway, he got weird and was too cool for me. He also brought another friend with him, and I hadn't had many to start with.

So, when my friends pretended they didn't know me and I was suddenly alone at a new school, I decided I would try a new approach.

I found the only people who would accept me for me. That's why I looked like this when I was in middle school:

My new friends and I wore a lot of black and listened to Korn and Limp Bizkit. "In the nineties, we called them goths," James says like a seventy-year-old man. I do recall a couple times when the guys wore black nail polish. I never did the nail polish, but to each his own. I really didn't judge them. Obviously, they were the nicest people to me, and it made lunchtime less lonely, but I can't say that I was being genuine when I pretended to be into the music I co-headphoned to with Alex. (I don't know for sure if his name was Alex, but I'm pretty sure it started with an A or an F, or maybe an M or an L. It could have been a D. Definitely not a Q or a B.)

I started finding my ground, discovering who I really was, and in this case, who I really wasn't. For the first time, I opened my mind to being myself first, and letting true friends follow. I grew apart from the goths, as beloved as they were to me in my time of need, and found friends that shared similar interests. I found a girl that I like-liked, and we would hug every day between the same two classes as we passed. Those were an exciting three weeks. Things started getting better, though they certainly were never perfect.

I still tended to treat everyone the same way I felt: like a loser. I could turn to my family for help and comfort, but they weren't perfect, and I didn't always treat them great. As much as they loved me, some days they couldn't really be there for me the way I needed.

Whether it's family, books, music, hobbies, or whatever gives you a source of strength, they are never perfect. The only perfect thing is the truth—the actual truth, not your personal truth. And by personal truth, I mean that we often assume things are a certain way, but since we know so little, we are wrong 99 percent of the time. I'm not talking about that time you had a nice cold drink of water on a hot day and said, "Mmm. This banana is delicious!" I mean all those negative things we tell ourselves and all the excuses we make for destructive behavior, and how every time we don't remotely understand what someone is explaining to us and they ask if it makes sense, we go, "Uh-huh."

If *your* truth is failing, figure out how it differs from the *actual* truth. This is a lifelong pursuit. It's a process of trial and error, and it takes a lot of humility (a.k.a. being wrong). The following are just a few things that have taken a long time for me to discover that are always true, no matter the situation:

- You have infinite, unchanging, enduring, absolute, non-negotiable value.
- You have the power to choose happiness or choose misery.
- You have gifts that you are meant to share with others.
- Your life has endless purpose, and you get to decide which purposes to pursue, whether one at a time or a hundred at a time.
- You will be okay, and it is always worth moving forward, whether you are running or barely moving one step.

Tough times can make you question your value. You need to know that you are worth it all the time, in nice or stormy weather. I had a way of making myself feel valuable, and it might sound funny, but it worked for me. It was a thought process that I went through to help me realize I had something to live for, and you may need something different. My thought process went something like this:

"Am I worth anything? Well, do I need to be worth anything? Does it matter? What about other people? Most of these people don't do all that much, yet they seem happy. I don't do all that much either. I've been happy before, why shouldn't I be happy again? If nothing else, I can smile at someone. I can make people laugh. It may not be worth much, but that guy playing Fortnite isn't doing much either. Einstein was a genius and he did more than most people for science, yet he said he felt insignificant like me. If we're all insignificant, then why am I so worried about it?"

It is usually good advice to not compare yourself to others, but for me, doing it in a positive way and comparing my present self to my past self helped me realize we're all in the same boat. I did have a choice to be happy. And I would soon feel better that I was only as inadequate as every other imperfect human. This may seem to con-tradict the idea of having a lot of potential, but paradoxically it takes the pressure off. It takes fulfilling your potential from being a chore to being an opportunity. You don't *have* to do anything, so you are *free* to do anything.

"And now that you don't have to be perfect, you can be good."
—John Steinbeck

The rest of this book is about freeing yourself from doing things that you *have to do*, and exploring who you truly are so you can create endless, spontaneous good. Have enough respect for yourself that you don't minimize who you are in order to temporarily and ineffectively please others. You will please others and yourself far more if you are genuine.

CAN GRATITUDE SAVE YOUR LIFE? CLICK HERE TO FIND OUT!

This last chapter in the *Stop Hitting Yourself* section is about loving your whole self, the universal self, which is you and the world around you.

Not to get too Deepak Chopra on you, but we are all connected to each other and to the universe. That's right, I said it. Deal with it. You have an effect on everyone and everything around you, because we all depend on the same laws of the universe. It's like the cells in your body. If one cell decides to rebel, it becomes cancerous and the whole body is affected. Every cell depends on every other cell, and their whole goal is to keep the body and each other alive. There is no master being or special cell that everyone is serving. It's the perfect example of complete community; they exist for each other, because of each other.

And what is the best way to show love for what you receive from your environment, your fellow beings, your world, and the universe? Gratitude!

Gratitude is not just saying what you are grateful for. It is a powerful, active perspective that helps you recognize how lucky you are to be a cell in the body of the universe, or the world, or your community, or your family, etc.

It's active because it requires you to care for the good around you. A person isn't grateful for their dog because they appreciate having a dog. They are grateful for their dog because they feed it and pet it and take it on walks. They aren't grateful for their job because they like making money. They are grateful when they do an honest day's work, remain genuine in professional relationships, and kick the marketing guy's trash in ping pong for the joy of it, for example. That's how you know I was grateful for my engineering job. It's on my resume.

Kevin Clayson wrote a book called *Flip the Gratitude Switch*, where he helps you unleash the power of gratitude for any situation, especially what you would normally call negative situations.[8] If you stub your toe walking out your front door, instead of screaming at someone, say, "I'm so glad I have a front door to stub my toe on. This is the first time in weeks I've stubbed my toe. Once this pain dies down, I have no other pain." And you can go on forever about the positive things that come from stubbing your toe. It isn't just accepting the bad; it is turning the bad into good.

Once, my wife bought an ugly couch. It was yellow and the fabric was uncomfortable. It was a "cool" couch. I think Brenna was being "hip" when she bought it. Or, the more likely case, she has better taste than me and I can only handle soft, grey couches with big pillows. I'm a simple man.

Gratitude saved the day. The truth about this situation is we had two couches. It meant I was in a situation where I could have two couches, and only one of them was ugly. It meant I had a family room big enough to hold two couches. It meant I have a wife that takes the time to look for good deals on couches, and tries to add some style to my life. I have a free interior designer! A couple years later, when we were moving to a place where the couch wouldn't work, she sold that couch for three times what she bought it for. Shows you what I know about what looks good: not much. By the way, my brothers and I all dress way better since I've been married. Brenna has really cleaned this family up.

If you think you've found a situation where gratitude can't pierce through the darkness, I challenge you to watch the TED Talk given by Valarie Kaur called "Three Lessons of Revolutionary Love in a Time of Rage."[9]

Valarie's uncle was the first man killed in response to 9/11 because he was Sikh. Not only are Sikhs not Muslim, but most Muslims are peaceful worshippers who are against radical ideas. Yet he and his family had to endure the devastating results of someone's ignorant violence. The family had every right to be furious. The family forgave the murderer, but they didn't forget the pain it brought or the joy her uncle had created during his life. His wife, when asked if she had anything to say to Americans, only said, "Three thousand Americans came to my husband's memorial. They did not know me, but they wept with me. Tell them thank you."[10]

She didn't have hate in her heart. She didn't take the opportunity to get back at anyone or get enveloped in rage. That would only have made the situation worse, and the situation was already tragic. Valarie is part of a community that campaigns for tolerance and peace. She said, "I looked back on all of our campaigns, and I realized that anytime we fought bad actors, we didn't change very much. But when we chose to wield our swords and shields to battle bad systems, that's when we saw change."[11]

She knew that fights against people are contentious and lead to destruction, but fights against ignorance and systems that allow injustice are always worth it and often effective. When we are grateful, even for the negative things in our lives, we stop fighting the little things that we think are in the way of our happiness. Instead, we fight the systems in our attitudes and the systems (also called habits) that ineffectively seek revenge where there is none to be had. We choose to be proactive and helpful, or we choose to be miserable.

And if it seems too hard to be grateful for all things because you know you can't stop yourself from feeling sad or angry, my advice is to stop trying to avoid sadness and anger. All of our emotions, including the difficult ones, are necessary for life, and none of them have the power to take away our peace. As Valarie became a mother, she discovered, "Mothering has taught me that all of our emotions are necessary. Joy is the gift of love. Grief is the price of love. Anger is the force that protects it."[12]

Life is totally unfair. Thank goodness! If life were fair, we would all suffer for every bad thing we've done. If life were fair, your imperfection would lead to devastation, because you would never be able to do anything perfectly, and that would ruin your life. You would pay for every sin, and you would have to earn goodness before you could experience it. Do you think in your darkest days, when you are most in need of love, that you would have the strength and courage to go out and earn it? I wouldn't. Yet, people have come to me most in my darkest hours, when I least deserved it. I'm so glad life is so much kinder than it is fair.

When you want the world to be "fair," you are saying you need to be given something. We've already talked about how it isn't what you are given that makes you happy. Be grateful for what you are given, and then everything you have or don't have becomes a gift. And since "everything you have or don't have" pretty much encompasses everything in existence, you can see how powerful gratitude really is. If you would rather be anyone other than yourself, you need a new perspective.

I used to really want to be Johnny Depp. He had an amazing career in acting doing parts that looked really fun to me: Willy Wonka in *Willy Wonka and the Chocolate Factory*, The Mad Hatter in *Alice in Wonderland*, Sweeney Todd in—you guessed it—*Sweeney Todd*. But sure enough, eventually I realized that someone with facial hair that creepy must have hard things going on in their life. JK, Johnny, you do you. Everyone has his or her own ups and downs. I'm just grateful my ups and downs are meant for me.

THIS TAKES TIME

If you have ever done a workout, you know it takes time before you get stronger. In fact, it hurts before it ever feels good. You don't get mentally buff overnight either. Take time to put these things into practice, and when you mess up, just learn from it. This is truly a lifetime pursuit.

Go easy on yourself. I am far from being great at these things, but I know when I make them a priority, I start getting stronger and happier. My life goes more smoothly and I am better prepared to apply the principles of the next three sections: Find Your Style, Collaborate, and Play Hard.

Go do something nice for yourself real quick,
and I'll see you in the next section.

NOTES

1. "Total Surface Area Required to Fuel the World with Solar," Land Art Generator Initiative, August 3, 2009, https://landartgenerator.org/blagi/archives/127.
2. Widely attributed to Kurt Cobain or Marilyn Monroe.
3. Amy Cuddy, "Your Body Language May Shape Who You Are," presented June 2012 at TEDGlobal, TED video, https://www.ted.com/talks/amy_cuddy_your_body_language_shapes_who_you_are#t-51395.
4. Kendall E. Matthews, "How to Read Body Language in Less Than 30 Seconds," http://www.kendallmatthews.com/how-to-read-body-language/.
5. Tony Bancroft and Barry Cook, dir. *Mulan*, Disney, 1998.
6. Isaac Lidsky, "How Can Going Blind Give You Vision?" interview by Guy Raz, NPR, January 19, 2017.
7. Isaac Lidsky, "What Reality Are You Creating for Yourself?" presented June 2016 at TEDSummit, TED video, 7:04, https://www.ted.com/talks/isaac_lidsky_what_reality_are_you_creating_for_yourself.
8. Kevin Clayson, *Flip the Gratitude Switch* (Gratifuel, LLC, 2016).
9. Valarie Kaur, "3 Lessons of Revolutionary Love in a Time of Rage," presented November 2017 at TEDWomen, TED video, https://www.ted.com/talks/valarie_kaur_3_lessons_of_revolutionary_love_in_a_time_of_rage.
10. Ibid., 7:27.
11. Ibid., 14:50.
12. Ibid., 16:39.

Tip 2:
Find Your Style

style

/ˈstaɪl/

noun

1. The way you do stuff.
2. What makes you feel like yourself.

Origin

The first fish to emerge from the water and evolve into a land species was depressed, so it went to its shark friend and said, "I'm done with this whole water thing that everyone is into. It's so stale." And the shark couldn't hear very well, because it's hard to talk under water, so it said, "It's style?" and the fish said, "Not my style!" And the fish walked on land and found its purpose in life.

Example

"My parents want me to be an elephant trainer, but that's not my style."

synonyms: your true self, your art, your weirdness, tastefully colorful socks, what Rihanna wears.

I was a teenager once.

You know how everyone deals with the stresses of being a teenager in different ways? Some kids are rebellious and some are strictly obedient. Some are very stressed and some never seem to think more than ten seconds into the future. Some like to do dangerous things, and some like to sit in their own room and never talk to anyone. I've tried to think of what my coping style was when I was a kid, and the best I've come up with is what I'm calling Constructive Rebellion.

Constructive Rebellion is where you think you are rebellious, but you're really too terrified to disobey any actual rules. For instance, in our house growing up, my parents would make sure we finished our homework before we could go to a friend's house or play games. So when my parents asked, "As long as you got your homework done. Is it done?" instead of lying to them and saying I already did it, I rebelled against the idea that I had to do my homework *in a timely manner*. I'm pretty hardcore.

With my rebellious attitude, I said, "It's not done yet. I'm doing my homework at 5 a.m. tomorrow."

"Really?"

"Yes, I need a break, okay?"

"Okay. As long as you get it done."

"I will! Gosh!"

So I slammed the door and went to my friend's house, then woke up at 5 a.m. the next day and did my homework. Ha! I showed them!

Because when you are afraid of getting in trouble, but you want to show adults you don't have to do what they say, you have to make up rules that aren't real, so you can break them.

Whichever kind of teenager you were or are, be it Constructive Rebel, Obedient Showoff, or Kid Who Accidentally Wears His Pants Backwards and Plays It Off Like He Did It on Purpose, you get a glimpse into your own style. There is a reason you do things differently from your siblings and friends. In fact, living your purpose depends on you embracing that difference.

Of course, there is way more to you than just one label, which is where this section comes in handy. You're like a painting, and you have many colors and textures and stuff. Actually, you're more interesting than that, because paintings are fun for like two minutes tops. You are like Bruce Wayne's warehouse of gadgets. You have amazing tools that no one else has, and every time you take on a new challenge, you get introduced to new ones.

Section one gave you tools to believe you can and should live your dream. Now it's time to start living it! You have the potential of the sun, and this section helps you discover how to use all that energy. If you are going to bless the world in a unique way that no one else could, then you should probably know what is unique about you. I call it *Finding Your Style*.

It's a lot more fun too. Figuring out the one special thing you are supposed to do in life is so stressful. What if you get it wrong? What if you're too late, and you won't be as good at it as you would have been had you discovered it on time? I'm getting stressed out just thinking about it.

But there is no such thing as being you incorrectly. You can't be too late to being yourself. Your self is always there waiting to be discovered.

I call it *Finding Your Style* because "style" denotes your way of doing something, what you like, how you express yourself, and how you leave your mark. Instead of just knowing who you are, it's about knowing how you influence the things and people around you. It requires that you do something. You can't sit there *thinking* about your talents with style, but you can go out and *express* your talents with style.

No longer will you try to discover some singular purpose that you go out and work on for eight hours a day, only to come home and "do whatever" until you get back to your purpose. You will find your style that you will apply to everything you do. The way you talk to people, the way you sing, the way you learn, the way you work, and even the way you stand in line at the grocery store could all be influenced by your style.

If *Stop Hitting Yourself* gave you the power and confidence to do good things, then *Finding Your Style* will help you know what those good things should be. Then you'll be on your way to living your dream.

EVERYTHING IS ART

My wife is super Irish. I only say super because all Irish people, or descendants of Irish people, are super Irish. No one I know of Irish descent is just a little bit Irish. You will never meet an Irish person on St. Patrick's Day and wonder, "Hmm. I'm not sure if that person is Irish."

Brenna, my lovely Irish girl, makes a full, celebratory Irish dinner on St. Patrick's Day, and it is one of my favorite things. Last year, she was in the early stages of pregnancy and feeling sick, so we decided not to invite everyone over for the great dinner. I figured she would take it easy that day, and maybe we would just have a simple corned beef. Nope. She still cooked the soda bread, baked potatoes, cabbage, and Greaney ginger cake to go with it. It just meant more for us. Clever girl. (By the way, if you don't know what Greaney ginger cake is, you live a sad existence and I pity you.)

We attend every St. Patrick's Day event we can find time for, and I can't wait for my daughter to be grown up in this very Irish environment, only to become just as staunchly Irish, waving the same "Erin Go Bragh" flag in front of her house.

I only have one issue with Brenna's traditions. Every year, she makes me watch the most obnoxious movie, just because it takes place in Ireland. She usually has great taste in movies, so I don't understand why she watches this terrible rom-com every year. There are plenty of Irish movies Brenna could choose to watch, but for some reason she always makes sure to watch *P.S. I Love You.*

Don't get me wrong; I am a fan of rom-coms. I love a well-written, well-cast rom-com as much as the next guy. (Can we stop pretending guys don't love them too?) But in this movie, the two main characters have no chemistry, and neither one has that charm that makes you root for them.

But there is one thing the main girl says that I think is really cool. She is talking about art (very awkwardly to the guy, who is listening awkwardly), and she says, "It doesn't matter if it's a work of art, or a taco, or a pair of socks! Just create something . . . new, and there it is, and it's you, out in the world, outside of you."[1] Then it's ruined by the guy's cheesy response and you're taken out of a cool moment and I hate the movie.

It doesn't matter if it's a taco, or a pair of socks, or this award-winning book. It is you. Everything you do or say can be a reflection of you, or it can be a counterfeit, depending on if you are acting genuinely. When it is a genuine reflection of you, it can be considered art. Then everything you do is beautiful.

WHAT A WASTE OF A PERFECTLY GOOD WASTE OF TIME

I used to worry a lot about wasting time. I didn't want to fail to do what it took to be successful, and for me success didn't mean too much. It just meant that I was happy, secure, loved, totally at peace, free, able to give back, in love with my job, never worrying about money, always healthy, a unicorn, one of the great scientific minds of the twenty-first century, a one-of-a-kind artist, also Oscar-winning but didn't have a speech prepared because of how unexpected it was, traveling because I would live humbly but that's the one thing I would splurge on, eating great food because that's the one thing I would splurge on, and holding parties for friends and family to gather together because that's really the one thing I want to splurge on. No pressure, right?

It's easy to get caught up in what we think we need, and therefore easy to stack things on our to-do list to meet our growing expectations. So, we have a culture of scheduling time efficiently and packing as much "doing" into our day as we can.

This doesn't leave much room for play, and what's the point of life being a game if we can't play it? What are you working so hard for if you aren't living your dream today? I don't believe in a life where you work for tomorrow. I believe in a life where you play hard today, and that creates a better tomorrow. That way today is a fun, challenging adventure that you can look back on with fondness, and tomorrow is a world full of opportunities to build on what you did today.

I discovered this better philosophy on life because I found myself lost in working for tomorrow, but tomorrow never came. There is no guarantee you will get tomorrow. Nothing outside of yourself is guaranteed. You could spend all your time earning and hoarding money and then an accident takes it all away. You could work up the corporate ladder and then get fired, or the company could go out of business. There are so many ways in which your environment can change, and though you may influence it, you don't have control.

Some people think this is terrible news, but I think it's the most freeing thought. If you can't control all of this stuff, that automatically means you *don't have to*! Do you really want to be in control of every aspect of your life? You, an imperfect person, required to make sure everything goes right? *That* would be terrible news.

This means that everything you do is bonus. Everything you do is just a way to make the world better. You get to partake in this world that is kinder than it is fair, getting far more than you can earn on your own, and your purpose in life is to add to it in a unique way that no one else could. You are like a light bulb plugging yourself into the circuit of the universe. The only way a light bulb glows is by receiving energy and then giving everything it receives. It's the flow of give *and* take that makes life bright, not the taking.

But James! If I can't control anything, what's the point of doing anything?!

First of all, stop yelling at me. Second, no one actually wants to do nothing.

As an example of how miserable it is to do nothing, ask my brother, Anthony, how fun it was to stand perfectly still for hours on end. Anthony was in the Marines, and his assignment was to do the dancing with guns for the president. It is much more dignified than that sentence makes it sound.

Part of his training was to actually stand in one spot for multiple hours without moving. He would have to wiggle his toes to avoid passing out, because people would actually pass out from standing too long. It was not enjoyable.

You don't want to do nothing, but you do want to waste time, and you want to do it effectively. We tend to think that any time we aren't purposefully achieving something we are "wasting time." Some of the best work I do is inspired by things that happen when I'm not working. My most popular character on Studio C came about because I was talking to Jason in a weird voice, throwing out a bunch of words, and when I said "bisque" he laughed. The whole sketch was built around that. You need to get out of your head in order to get out of the way of your own creativity.

It may seem like a cliché, or it may seem antiquated, or maybe it seems obvious, but nature has a magic to it. There is wisdom and intelligence in nature that rubs off on you when you do nothing but spend time in nature. People-watching isn't too far off, if you do it without judgment. Just observe and don't make judgments, whether in people-watching or in nature walking, and you'll gain way more insight.

Nature can teach us. We often make the mistake of thinking words are the only thing that teach us. How can we learn something if it is not explained to us? If you were ever a baby (and many of you were), you learned by observing and doing. You learned right and wrong, you learned safe and dangerous, and you learned communication skills, all without understanding a word your parents were saying. Don't be fooled into thinking you can't learn just by observing and letting your mind make connections. As a babies grow to adulthood, they can certainly learn more nuanced and complex concepts through words. Words are powerful, but so is instinct. Don't get caught up in trying to *understand* everything.

According to the Australian philosopher and poet Franz Kafka, you maybe don't even need nature. He said, "You need not leave your room, remain sitting at your table and listen. You need not even listen, simply wait. You need not even wait, just learn to become quiet, and still, and solitary."

We are built to be creative. It is our natural state. We stop being creative when we get in the way of what our minds want to do. Watch a child play, and you will see them create spontaneously. This should be the case when we waste time. Don't get distracted by stress, fear, and impatience. Let your thoughts and feelings guide you to new inspiration without force and without judgment. Deepak Chopra said, "As you gain more and more access to your true nature, you will also spontaneously receive creative thoughts."[2]

He makes a good point. We have infinite potential and creativity if we let it come, and we should trust our instincts when we feel something is good to pursue.

Spontaneous thoughts of creativity come because of you being you. Trying to be someone else will hinder the process.

I do a lot of scripture reading. I love it, but it isn't always the most riveting storytelling, and sometimes my mind starts to wander. I get halfway down the page and I don't know what I read, because my thoughts have gone on a different path. I used to make a huge mistake; I would go back and reread the page, trying to focus on the text this time.

It was a mistake because the thoughts that got me off track are often far more inspiring for my personal life. I think it puts my mind into a creative and inspired state and I shouldn't mess with it. Those thoughts are me and going back to reread is me trying to be someone else. So if I'm inspired by something totally off topic while reading scripture, I don't fight it anymore! That doesn't mean all of my random thoughts are diamonds, but that's okay. So, if a thought comes, go with it if it feels inspiring, ditch it if it feels stressful or materialistic.

If you're wasting time effectively, you will be excited to get to work on what inspires you. Then you can be self-motivated to roll up your sleeves and work hard, and that makes for a good day.

PAY ATTENTION AND STUFF

"We detect, rather than invent, our missions in life."

—Victor Frankl

When I was zero years old, I wasn't worried about my purpose in life. I wasn't thinking about preparing for the future, so I had no reason to figure out what it was I wanted. I couldn't even talk to anyone about it, because I didn't know what language was. This is the way I knew I wanted something: I saw it, and for some unknown reason, I liked it.

This chapter is about how to make better use of the skills of observation we all used as zero-year-olds. Don't assume you are good at this just because you used to be zero. As we grow older, we let a lot of things get in the way of our nature. We learn social rules that make us think we have to be a certain way or please certain people. We learn fear that says the world is a lonely, brutal place and failure is wrong. While fear and social rules have their place, we shouldn't let them get in the way of finding our style.

We do have an advantage over zero-year-olds, though, and that is the ability to focus our efforts. If we are patient and calm enough to observe something, just as we used to do, we can choose to remember it. We can delve into that interest. We can write it down and think about it later. We can talk to other people about it and expand our understanding of it. We can intentionally practice it and hone our skills.

When I was a teenager, my brother Troy was really interested in airplanes. He enjoyed studying physics because he could learn how airplanes worked. At sixteen years old, he took lessons to learn how to pilot a plane. For a few weeks, I heard something about Troy flying planes, but I was too focused on my angst to pay attention, until the day he had his first solo flight.

When I saw him get in the plane and fly in the air, it finally hit me that my brother could fly a plane. So, I got really curious. Why was Troy flying a plane? I thought people who liked planes just read books about it or used their tickets at the arcade to get those weak little airplane kits that break on the first flight. Normal people don't fly planes; pilots fly planes. What, Troy just decided he wanted to fly a plane, and now he's flying a plane?

Then it hit me: *I think Troy just decided he wanted to fly a plane, and now he's flying a plane.*

I suddenly realized I could just decide I wanted to do something, and I could do it. If anyone else had ever done it before, why couldn't I do it? If no one else had done it before, why couldn't I still do it? No one in our family had ever flown a plane, and there Troy was, terrifying my mother to his heart's content.

I had heard many times that I could "be anything" and I should "reach for the sky," but I didn't really believe it until I saw my brother fly. It has to be true, because it rhymes.

We have rules about ourselves that we didn't choose. "I can't do that because I'm too young." "I can't love that music/movie/hobby because that's for losers." "I have to get a certain type of job, because only those people are successful and happy." Like Pavlov's dog, we are conditioned to those fears and social rules, and we don't realize we should instead make rules for ourselves. What if the rules we follow came from our own experience and choice?

A rule should only be made if breaking it makes life worse.

In *Positive Discipline*, author Jane Nelsen has an awesome chapter called "Natural and Logical Consequences."[3] It builds on this idea that rules aren't made out of nowhere; they come from our true nature. She gives an example of figuring out how to get a child to eat food they don't want to eat, without forcing rules on them that they would rebel against or that would require you to threaten them. The kids weren't getting ready for school on time, so she used the natural consequence of hunger. She had a family meeting where they decided that breakfast was from 8:00 to 8:30, and no one could eat after 8:30. Sure enough, one of her kids showed up at 8:31, and he got no breakfast. He threw a tantrum the first time, but after the second time a couple weeks later, she never had a problem with kids being ready on time.

So it is with our personalities. We are unique, and discovering the rules that govern that uniqueness requires that we pay attention to how we respond to things. As a simple example, if you consistently go to bed at midnight and consistently wake up tired, you should recognize that a natural rule for you might be that you should go to bed earlier. My wife knows that a rule for her is to stop talking after 11 p.m.; otherwise, she can't wind down. That's not true for me, so it took me a while to stop ruining her sleep with my endless ranting about what the best type of chocolate is.

This should apply to your interests as well. If you try painting, and you consistently find that you are relaxed and peaceful afterward, that gives you insight into something that relaxes you and brings you peace. So you make a rule that when you don't want to feel relaxed and peaceful, you make sure to not paint.

To further investigate this concept, let's look at two possibilities of what might happen when you try to make money off of those paintings.

Possibility 1: As you try to figure out how to price your paintings and where to sell them, it starts stressing you out, and every time you paint, you have dollar signs in your head and it isn't relaxing anymore. It even messes with your creativity, and you aren't happy with what you create. You want all animals in your paintings to have three eyes, but the world just can't accept your originality. They just don't get the symbolism! Then you know you should stop trying to make money off of it.

Possibility 2: Having a deadline and potential buyer might be your style, and might even inspire you. One day someone emails you exactly what they would want in a painting, and you decide to paint it for them. You discover you're inspired by painting things that are meaningful to others. Not only do you now have a stream of income, but maybe you also discovered a great personal gift when Christmas comes around—painting things that are meaningful to others. I mean, it's better than fruit cake. Unless your passion is fruit cake, in which case you might be the person who figures out how to make people want to eat it.

It's really just trial and error, but pay attention to what you learn. It is also crucial that you remember to be genuine. For example, I have wasted so much effort, even during trial and error, because I was too worried about money to let something be a hobby. The instant I had the idea that I could make money off of it, I turned it into a stressful situation.

For example, I really enjoy woodworking. I love that I can make so many things, including things that people actually use, and put some skill and artistry into it. What a great hobby! But there have been a few times where I wanted to turn it into a way to make some extra money on the side. This might lead to an awesome career for some, but for me it needed to remain a hobby.

I found that trying to make money with it was super stressful, but saving money was totally fine for me. Making money involves customers and prices and business expenses and all this new stuff I don't want to deal with. But saving money is fine, because I'm not usually in a hurry to get some new furniture, so I can take my time with it and enjoy the process. Also, I have a good excuse to buy a new tool, because I'm saving money by making it myself. #DadLife

Money, of course, isn't the only false rule we obey.

Let's say you learn that you love making pastries. You imagine all your friends tasting your delicious treats and asking you if you're bringing some of your amazing pastries to the next gathering. You play coy, but then you show up to the Oscar party with little black bow ties on your perfectly baked croissants, and this time you don't care how poorly you do on Oscar bingo, because who's winning the award for best snack tonight? You are!

Sorry, I got lost in the story. But imagine how terrible it would be if you gave that up because you think desserts are shameful, so you just give up altogether. I believe in being healthy, but I also believe in balance. What if you really loved math, but you didn't pursue it because someone says it isn't cool? What if you want nothing more than to be a stay-at-home dad, but your culture makes you feel guilty for not making more money than your wife?

These are real false rules we get stick on. Real false doesn't make sense, but you know what I mean. They are *legitimate* false rules, and whether they come from society or our fears, they are very hard to overcome. But you can do something small to push yourself in the right direction, and you never know how far you'll be able to go. You don't have to completely change your life to live a little more genuinely.

The good news is that your happiness matters more than society's expectations, and nothing significant is going to happen to rob you of that genuine happiness. The only person holding you back in all of these situations is you.

That's why Finding Your Style is such a crucial step in living your dream, because you are always open to new experiences. These experiences lead to finding out what rules govern your own happiness, and you'll actually want to discipline yourself to follow them, because you are motivated by real consequences. So really, in order for rules to work, they can't be made—they have to be discovered.

In the next section, we'll talk a lot about following the opportunities that match your style. The more you explore your style, the more ways you will find you can adapt it to the opportunities that come. There is no end to making your life and the lives of everyone around you better. If you want to paint three-eyed horses climbing trees to gather freshly picked iPads, you do you!

Insights can come at unexpected times, so you'd better be paying attention. I had to apply to college while I was on a mission in Italy. The mission was a busy time and I didn't have a lot of free time to figure out what major to apply for, but it was in the back of my mind.

An opportunity came for us to do some service cleaning up the yard of the local church in Mestre. Since every day consisted of walking around, knocking on doors, and trying to talk to people who didn't want to talk to me, getting down in the dirt and doing some manual labor sounded wonderful. I could just focus on making a yard beautiful, and no one could reject me. I grew up helping out in the yard, and though I wouldn't say it was fun, I had to admit it was satisfying to see the results of my work. Now that I had been away from home for more than a year, this felt like home. It was nice to do something I felt successful at.

I assumed everyone felt this way. Who wouldn't want to take a break from getting turned away and get in touch with nature (kind of)? I was on my knees, lost in the bliss of weed pulling, when I looked up and saw that the other missionaries were much less interested. It dawned on me that I was unique in this feeling. I was proud of my work, as insignificant as it may have been to most people, and it meant something to me that I was accomplishing something I liked.

Soon after that, the deadline for applying to college came up. My mind was too occupied with the mission to really get deep into figuring out what major to apply for, but I had recently had this revelation about my love for landscaping. So I applied to BYU through the landscape management major, and I got in. Yay!

Like I said in my story, I ended up changing it once I actually got to college, but to this day I still love doing landscaping. It may not be what I studied, or what I do for my job, but even my friends know me as a gardener. It's one of the many reasons why I'm actually a seventy-year-old man in a thirty-year-old's body. Another reason is that my dream car is a Toyota Avalon: large, smooth ride, quiet, and comfortable. None of that juvenile sports car stuff for me; I might spill my Ovaltine!

You can learn a lot by observing your past. If you're human, most of your life growing up, you didn't pay much attention to what you were doing; you just did things. If you can look back on what you did, you can gain some good insight into your style, because some things don't change. If you have a terrible memory like me, you can ask friends and family about what you loved or what you paid attention to or talked about a lot. You could even ask what was weird about you, because if you were doing something different from other kids, it probably came from your weird, unique self, and maybe that's just what the world needs.

You may have even been paying attention at the time, but you have just forgotten. You know, like a journal. I wrote in my journal religiously for only two years, my junior and senior years of high school.

I have some journal entries before and after that, but I was prolific during those two years. Once I sift through all the raging hormones, I rediscover some fascinating things about what mattered to me.

It's a cool way to get to know yourself, because with enough writing samples you can see patterns pop up. You can set aside sentences like, "Dinner was good. We had hamburgers. I want another one." Those will always be there, because journal writing is very stream-of-consciousness stuff (at least mine was, to a fault). The important stuff tends to come up in a way you wouldn't have noticed in the moment. Reading the journal as a whole, you begin to see that it was an important subject for you. It isn't too late to start writing in a journal. You should do it now, because after a few months of writing, you can look back at it as a whole and notice the patterns that show up currently, even if you are having a hard time figuring out in the moment.

This all requires that we don't be stuck in our ways. Julian Treaure, whose profession is, I kid you not, a sound consultant (talk about finding a unique purpose), gave a TED Talk called "Five Ways to Listen Better." He said, "We're losing our listening"[4] and "We've become desensitized. Our media have to scream at us with these kinds of headlines [Revealed! Scandal! Exposed! etc.] . . . And that means it's harder for us to pay attention to the quiet, the subtle, the understated."[5]

When you're finding your style, pay attention to quiet things. Make an effort to notice what others don't notice, and listen where others don't listen, so you can learn what others don't learn and live the dream most people don't live.

ONE MAN'S TRASH IS ANOTHER MAN'S "STRENGTHS"

I feel like every time you talk to someone about what to do with your life, they ask you, "What are your strengths?" Then you list off a bunch of uninteresting answers, like "I work well with people" or "I'm a hard worker" or "I know how to say words real good." You often end up with a list full of "strengths" that are basically required for anyone to be a normal person.

The other question they might ask is, "What things do you like to do?" This would usually make me think, "I like to sleep, eat, play games, hang out with friends, not do my homework, etc." There are plenty of things we like to do, but not all of them result in accomplishment or fulfillment.

The issue with these questions is that they focus on what you *already* do. If what you already do is the answer, then you're already doing it. Problem solved. But you're looking for growth. You want something that interests you but that also requires growth and results in something you are proud of.

So, instead of asking yourself, "What are your strengths?" you should ask, "What do you want your strengths to be?"

This takes the focus off of choosing some particular job and puts the focus on how you would want to contribute uniquely to any job. You have greater flexibility to choose different jobs, because you know you can put your style into many different jobs.

Instead of being limited by what you are already good at, you use passion and inspiration to make plans for your future. For example, if you are really good at knitting, but you're not interested in doing it, you can ignore all those calls from high-end knitting schools offering you full-ride scholarships. Many opportunities may come in life that are not genuine to you, so don't be afraid to say no to things when you feel strongly that they are not for you. But maybe you start noticing you are very interested in the costumes when you watch movies (because you have read my book and started paying more attention—you're welcome). So, you start talking to local wardrobe artists. You try out a few simple designs and decide you want to do harder ones. One of those local artists likes you and needs some weekend help, so you help them and find out you love the work. You keep doing it for fun on the side, while paying the bills with your day job, and a year later you get a call from a colleague of that wardrobe person you worked with. They want you to help with a three-month project, and it's a paid gig.

Now, at this point (just like any point in life) a million things could happen. You could make costuming a career, you could never do it again, you could do it as a hobby, you could do something related, and so on. The future is full of surprises, and you can try to make plans, but the opportunities that will present themselves are endless and usually unpredictable. All you know today is that you are following your truth. When the opportunities do come, be open to new things and be excited to go beyond your comfort zone. In the end, you never could have predicted where you would be, but you prepared yourself for opportunities that are good for you by doing what was good for you all along.

You never know where inspiration will strike. When I was a freshman in high school, I had to choose an elective. I was given a choice of ten or so classes to choose from, and woodshop stood out to me. I had zero experience making things out of wood, but I liked working with my hands, so I gave it a try.

Our main assignment for the semester was to build a mirror. I think the only requirements were that it had a wood frame and needed to fit a specific size mirror. It sounded like the most boring assignment to me. Maybe I had chosen the wrong elective. So, I decided to apply my style to it and make it more interesting. I decided to make my mirror frame the shape of a guitar.

There is no reason why I would have the skills to make a guitar-shaped mirror frame, when the rest of the class was expected to basically make a rectangle over the entire semester. But I thought it was a cool idea, so I did it. It made me interested in something that I otherwise thought was boring, so it made me do it better that I would have done. Even my shop teacher told me I couldn't do it. He said it was too complicated and too advanced for my skill level, so I just upped my skill level. When you care about something, your strengths do not matter. The only thing that matters is that you keep caring about it and working at it. The point of finding your style is to set your path toward things that are as close as possible to what you care about, so everything you do is done well and with pride.

My guitar mirror is still alive today, over fifteen years later. It recently hung in my brother Greg's house, either because he is proud of me or because he's cheap and doesn't want to spend money on other decorations. He did recently ask me if I want him to give it to me or throw it away, but I think it's because his new wife has too many decorations and he would be too jealous to have it hang in anyone else's house. Greg appreciates my artistry.

Austin Kleon wrote a book called *Steal Like an Artist*,[6] and I'm going to steal one of his ideas. One of his methods for being creative is to pick out a few people or things that inspire you, then take pieces of

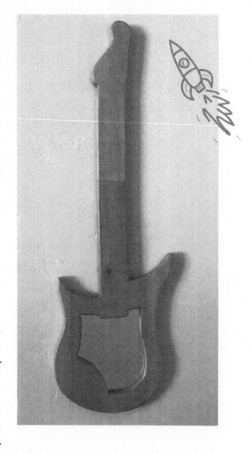

each of those and combine them. What you end up with is something completely unique to you. No one else would have used that exact combination of inspirations and combined them the same way you did.

I think the same process should apply to discovering who we are. Take all the things in the world you love, all the people who inspire you, and group them together. Think about why you love those things in particular. Something about who you are draws you to those things, because each piece is a reflection of a piece of you. Therefore, the combination of all those pieces together makes you you.

I have a couple writing styles that are different from anyone else on Studio C. As someone who studied engineering, my analytical side comes out in the way I format my sketches, whereas other writers write very intuitively. When I'm not analytical, I seem to revert to the childhood personality my mom pointed out to me, and my writing is more akin to a cuddly child eating dirt: completely absurd, but adorable. Everyone has their own styles that make the group more well-rounded.

So don't decide your purpose based on what your strengths are, but instead what you want your strengths to be: a reflection of what you love. In fact, if everyone only did what they were already good at, the human race would end, because no one would become parents.

Don't wait until you are good at something to get started. Fake it till you make it. I had to learn as I went when I made that guitar mirror. I had to learn as I went with sketch comedy, but that didn't stop me from doing it. Thank goodness I didn't wait until I was good before I auditioned, because I definitely wouldn't be on Studio C. Learning as you go is one of the best ways to learn, and it's more fun than reading about it.

There is no perfection in any effort. We know this logically, but we forget this in the moment, and we hesitate to do anything until we have every assurance that we will succeed. I love Elizabeth Gilbert's quote in her book *Big Magic*: "Done is better than good."[7]

Now I know that last quote was from a book, but don't wait until you've read every book on the subject before you try.

Books are amazing resources for knowledge and guidance, and you should read many of them, but there are so many books on every subject these days that you'll be dead before you finish them. Even if you finish the last one right before you die, someone will have just published another one, and your last words will be cursing their name from the old decrepit chair you haven't removed yourself from in fifty years. What a life.

You'll actually remember better what you learned in your reading if you work along the way. Imagine reading your entire school textbook, and not starting on your first assignment until you finished. How much would you remember? If you're a human, you would probably do very poorly on that assignment. If you're a robot, you would remember everything, but this book isn't for you. You want to know your purpose, robot? GET BACK TO VACUUMING MY FLOORS, ROOMBA! But I digress.

In short, knowledge is great but not really worth much until you put it into practice. So, read a little to get started, but as soon as you can start making any progress, get to work. As I always say, done is better than good.

FAKE IT TILL YOU MAKE IT

This entire book came from asking questions. The only answers I am able to give came from asking questions over and over again, and gaining new insight every time I asked. As I continue to explore answers to these questions, more questions come up, and I hope that happens for you. Ask as many questions as you can. Write them down. Ponder them as you read this book and other books (but not too many! See above), listen to talks, listen to people, and observe life as it happens.

Kids are good at this. They ask questions all the time. They ask questions that we don't even have the answers to. Have you ever asked them in return, "I don't know, what do you think?" It's amazing the answers you get. They often have very insightful answers, even when they're wrong. These kids are practicing "fake it till you make it" and they're learning a lot from it.

It brings up another interesting point, which is that in the scheme of all knowledge and wisdom, we are as close to ignorance as a child. Whatever we may know or assume, there is so much we get wrong. One advantage we have over kids—and yet almost no one uses it as often as one should—is the ability to say what you think, take a step back, and say, "But is that really the way things are?" We move beyond just *reacting* to what is given to us, and we *act for ourselves* to purposely challenge our own false ideas and bad habits. If we don't take advantage of this self-reflection, we're acting like children and denying ourselves of life-changing insight and wisdom. We're acting like my ten-month-old daughter, who mistakenly believes that food has to be shoved into her hair before it can go into her mouth. That's just an unnecessary extra step for all of us. Grow up, June.

We have the power to learn the mysteries of life just by thinking about them. The power is there, regardless of where we think it comes from. I happen to believe this is a spiritual trait within us, that we are connected to God and that knowledge is available to us if we seek it. But even if you don't believe that, the power is still there and has been used by the greatest minds in human history.

Most of what Einstein did was a thought experiment. The more he thought about it, the more things started coming together, and he would often lay out a way for someone else to do the physical experiment to "prove" the validity of his theories.

STEP BY STEP

(ALSO A '90S TV SHOW, NOW AVAILABLE ON HULU)

I am terrified of ledges. Some people are afraid of heights, but this is different. I have no problem going on roller-coasters. In fact, I love roller-coasters. One of most fun things I have done was skydiving, and that plane is at a very high height when you jump out of it. So, no problem with heights or falling, since in both situations falling is the entire point.

Open ledges, however, are the worst. I can't even stand banisters. There is a walking bridge between the two sides of the BYU Broadcasting building that I have to cross every time I go to work. It has clear glass banisters, so it feels like there are no banisters. I get vertigo every time I walk across it. I had a banister at my house growing up, and no matter how many times I went up it, I would still lose my balance. My mind just freaks out and shuts off my body's balancing mechanisms. I can't walk anywhere near a cliff, because my brain will turn against me. If I attempted to, my brain would just be like, "How dare you?" and then turn my body 90 degrees and jump off.

My brother Troy always thought it was funny to run and jump over a banister when I was standing near it. He would actually hold the railing and flip upside down to the other side. I, of course, would cower away from the banister. I would crumple up in a ball and fall to the ground or just run the other way. Not cool, Troy!

It's not in my personality to live on the ledge.

I am currently a full-time actor and writer. I never expected to do this as a career, because it was too risky. I studied engineering in college. Obviously I was planning on a steady, forty-hour workweek kind of job. It felt safe. Financial security was a big deal for me. It still is a big deal. So choosing to pursue a career in entertainment had to happen differently for me than for some of my friends.

Many of my friends from high school that I grew up making movies with studied theater in college. Sometimes I wondered if I made the wrong choice to not study theater because I was too much of a wimp. I wasn't brave enough to make the leap, and I felt like I didn't deserve it, so I never thought it would happen. I chose what I thought would be the more stable career, because security was so important to me. I had no idea that doing comedy for fun would lead to a job. I just wanted a release from all the engineering. I was just taking the opportunities as they came, until eventually the opportunity for Studio C came.

I've been able to visit some of my high school friends after a few years. Some ended up in New York, one in Chicago, and I randomly ran into one in a Sears in Boise, Idaho. We are all doing various things in film and entertainment, and we all took totally different paths to get there. It has been so cool to sit down to lunch with them and talk about how we all ended up where we ended up. I was in New York performing with Divine Comedy after studying engineering, and my friends were in New York performing after studying theater and moving there. We had different paths, but we followed our dreams.

I got where I am in a way that felt doable, and you should too. Notice that I didn't say comfortable. You don't need to be comfortable. In fact, I talk a lot in section four about comfort being one of the worst goals you can have. But you do need to understand your pace and respect it. It's like riding a bike. It would be stupid to just jump on and assume you can pedal and steer and balance and shift gears and go fast all at once. It would also be stupid to never get on the bike and try it. Somewhere between those two extremes is your pace.

You'll be fast at some things and slow at others. You need to trust your pace and know that everything will turn out the best if you respect that pace. It's just a feeling thing. As you start to go faster than your mind and body can understand, you back off a little. And when you feel unchallenged, you'll get the urge to move up in skill.

I was slow at being an actor. It didn't mean I didn't deserve it. It didn't mean I was less worthy than my friends. It just meant I had to go at my own pace. Meanwhile, I was almost burning myself out with full-time school, two jobs, marriage, and Divine Comedy, but no one's perfect.

My wife and I often talk about how glad we are that we really *did* college. We were young and free and able to experience things and take it all in while we were young. Don't do so many things that you can't enjoy what you are doing. Every day is a chance to do things a little better than yesterday. What's the rush? Don't run faster than you have strength.

Here's an analogy about a tree.

Think about how a tree grows. It starts with just one trajectory: up. Once it is strong enough and can't get nutrients it needs from one stem, it branches out. Just a couple of branches go out. Those grow away from each other, exploring a couple different areas. Once they are strong in those areas, they branch out from there, and so on until you have a large beautiful tree, gathering nutrients from many sources, with a trunk that is strong enough to hold all of them. Imagine if that tree had to know every place it would branch out to before it started growing. It would shoot out hundreds of little branches into the sky and each would choke the next. They would remain weak and the first strong wind or average three-year-old boy would crush it. No way would it get anywhere near bearing fruit. And then there's no apple pie. You can see how the situation gets dire very quickly.

I want you to bear fruit. I don't want you to be a dumb little sea anemone that doesn't do anything for anyone. In other words, I don't want you to be a pretty little blob that terrifies children on their fifth-grade trip to the ocean. Unless you're an old man in a bikini, then you just let your freak flag fly and you scare those children like there's no tomorrow. (Sea anemone reading this: "I came here to have a good time and honestly I feel so attacked right now.") Anyway, back to the tree analogy.

Just like the tree, don't assume you need to know where you're going to be in twenty years, ten years, five years, or even next year. You can make plans, and you can start on a certain trajectory, but when you come up on an opportunity to expand, take the opportunity and enjoy seeing where it takes you. You know, like a tree branch.

Jim O'Doherty was a stand-up comedian. He claims he was a bad stand-up comedian. He wasn't making any money, but he loved what he was doing. One day, someone told him he would be good at warming up audiences at shows. When they film in front of a live audience in Hollywood, they always have someone warming up the audience, getting them ready to be an energized and active audience. He tried it out and loved it. He was pleasantly surprised to find they actually paid well enough to make it a career. So, here he was, doing a job he loved that he never even knew about before.

After years of working in TV (for instance, on the show *Married with Children*), someone told him he should be a writer. He was so funny warming up audiences that someone took the time to tell him he should write. He wrote an episode of *Married with Children*, and it did really well. He went on to write more episodes for that show, and he later helped develop *3rd Rock from the Sun*. These were huge shows, and he was enjoying a new career as a writer, something he had never planned on. He goes on to explain subsequent similar experiences, where he just did what he had to do "to survive" and it turned into the next step in his career.

Martin Short is one of the loveliest people on TV. I read his book, *I Must Say*,[8] where he talks about his path to stardom, and it is very similar to Jim O'Doherty's story. He started doing comedy because his friends were doing it and they said he was funny. One gig led to another until he started doing films. He had years of uncertainty, not knowing where his career would lead. But he just kept doing what he had to do to get by, meanwhile following his heart and taking opportunities as they came.

It seems that people who force their lives to fit their plan are often stressed and overwhelmed. They are fighting against the flow of opportunities coming their way that they are too blind to see, because they are so one-track minded. This doesn't mean you shouldn't work hard at something. The only way for opportunities to come is to be working hard. The key is to be open to opportunities that come from that hard work, to notice the natural offshoots that could turn into beautiful branches of your life tree.

It doesn't even mean we shouldn't want good things for ourselves. It is okay to work toward something material if it is something that will help you produce joy. My wife and I really love to cook and host friends and family. Now that we have a kid, the kitchen is suddenly so tiny. We have been looking for a long time for the next house, and the kitchen has been a huge motivator. Slowly but surely, miracle after miracle, we took a months-long journey that recently led us to finding the perfect place for our little family. Without going into detail, I'll just say we had so many plans of ways it could work out, and then an opportunity came that was better than anything we had planned. It's not like we needed a different kitchen to survive. There are billions of people with less than us. But we knew we would use it to bless our family and hopefully others, and I'll say it again, God is merciful.

Give plenty of time for things. They say when you're planning a project, think of how long you think it will take, then give yourself double that time. Things always come up that you didn't expect, and we tend to be less efficient in reality than we are in our minds. If you are rushing through everything you do, you can't enjoy what you are doing.

But James, what if I have so much to do that there is no extra time to go slow?

Do less.

It also gives you the time you need to continue finding your style. You don't want to be doing something inspiring and then be interrupted because you scheduled ten different life-changing activities in one afternoon. Plan to leave five to ten minutes early to your next thing, so when that time comes you have a couple minutes to slowly transition to the next thing. Then when you can't find your keys, you don't get so frustrated you kick your dog. I've never done that. My dog, Caesar, will never say I've done that. Because of the hush money.

ALL THE RIGHT REASONS
(ALSO A NICKELBACK ALBUM, NOW AVAILABLE ON SPOTIFY)

If you are upset that no one cares about your contribution, make sure you're doing it because you love it, because you believe in it. Your satisfaction shouldn't depend on other people approving of it. Anyone with a YouTube channel can tell you it's impossible, because no matter what you do, someone will dislike your video or make negative comments. There will also be people commenting "First Comment" because, as we all know, first comment is a great accomplishment.

Examine your motivations. Do it because it makes you happy or you believe the world needs more of it. Be kind to others because you believe in kindness, not because you want everyone to thank you or recognize your good deed. If you believe in kindness, you trust that your kindness makes life better, even if the person you meant to send that kindness to doesn't receive it with gratitude. That kindness goes up in the sky, and floats around, and eventually pops, and the remnants fall on some stranger's lawn and get caught in their lawnmower two days later. It's the circle of life. Or maybe that's balloons.

That goes for anything else you think is worth doing. Learn languages because it helps your brain, or because it brings culture into your life, or because it helps you understand people better, or a million other reasons. Write a blog because you want to express your feelings on a topic, or because you hate that topic, or because you hate Hot Topic.

In high school, my friend James Dugan and I built a boat for the boat regatta. I was not good at building boats, and neither was James, but we gave it our best. I designed it to look like a fishing boat, which apparently isn't the fastest type of boat. I thought it would go faster because of the speed flames I put on the front. The boats had to be made out of only cardboard and duct tape. So, I assumed the decorations had to be made out of duct tape as well. I actually cut out red, orange, and yellow pieces of duct tape to make flames on the front of the boat.

We didn't win the regatta. It was large and very buoyant, but it wasn't fast. I doubt the flames even helped. I named the boat *Brenna* after this cute girl at school. I later married that girl, so that gives you an idea of how sexy that boat was.

The original Brenna

The next year, we weren't going to be weighed down by a big ol' boat. We took a single cardboard box and turned it into perfection. Oars wouldn't weigh us down either. Instead, we depended on the strength of our legs. This meant we had to put four holes in the bottom of the boat for each of our legs, so we could run along the bottom of the pool.

We didn't win that time either. The bottom of the pool was further than the length of our legs. We kind of paddled around and ended up freestyle swimming with the boat caught between us, slowing us down. We called it the *Brenna 2* or the *B2 Bomber*.

The Brenna 2 *(or the* B2 Bomber*)*

I used to have the nagging thought that I should have done something differently in the past. When I was studying engineering, I was in classes with a lot people who had been into engineering-type stuff for years. Some had been working on cars since they were kids, some concurrently worked in machine shops, and some had been programmers for years.

I spent most of my teen years making movies and hosting pool parties. My dad was a computer guy, so I assumed it was the last thing I would want to do, and I never tried programming. I almost joined the mathletes, but according to the entrance exam, I was half a point too dumb. My brother Greg was really into working on cars, but I had no interest as a kid. When my parents saw my amazing guitar mirror, they got us a scroll saw. I made one thing with it.

I would talk to these people in class who had so much more experience than me and regret not doing those things as a kid. *I would be so much better now if I had started years ago. I would be so much more qualified for good engineering jobs and more ready to do good things in the world.* Stupid, immature me! I would even think, *I wish my parents would have made me do more!*

But this is all false thinking. It's not true that your parents should have made you practice this thing you are now in love with. You have to do it for your own reasons. Don't blame your parents for the fact that you don't have that path in life. There is no "falling behind" that you have to regret.

When I was fifteen, I decided I wanted to learn the piano. No one else was making me do it. I asked my parents if they would pay for lessons, and they said I could if I practiced every day. Of course I would practice—it was my idea to take the lessons. I did practice every day, and I improved really quickly. I was moving up levels faster than any of my teacher's other students, and I loved it.

The funny thing is my mom tried to get me to take piano lessons six years earlier. I practiced because I had to, and it wasn't very effective. I probably went about a year and didn't get very far. Honestly, it might have been a month, but it seemed like a year because I was so bored with it. No matter how much she wanted me do it, I was never going to be motivated until I did it for my own reasons. Maybe you are different from me and you thrive on parental encouragement, but remember I was a very rebellious child. My constructive rebellion made me *wait a few years* until I had my own reasons to do it. Sick burn!

Obviously, I don't regret wasting time making movies. It turned out I would have a job in film. But I couldn't see that at the time, so I spent too much time regretting my inability as a six-month-old to predict my future as an engineer.

Do you ever have regrets one day, but then the next day you find out it might be a good thing and suddenly you're glad you did things the way you did them? Then, fear creeps in again and starts telling you your whole life is over because of that stupid thing you did, and you should have done it the other way. Then the something comes to light and suddenly everything seems great. Soon enough a new piece of information makes you think, "Dang it! My life *is* over because of that thing!"

Whatever your insecurity is, be patient and try not to make rash decisions. Your genuine passion will come when you are ready to receive it, like my piano lessons, and engineering, and Studio C. Don't get all hung up and bent out of shape with "woulda, coulda, shouldas;" they're not helpful! Like the wise Pumbaa once said, "Put your behind in your past." You can't go back there and change one second of it, so do your best with what you have now and trust that it'll be great! From my experience, I think it'll be better for you the way it really happened. And if you're being genuine and living your style, you can be sure of that.

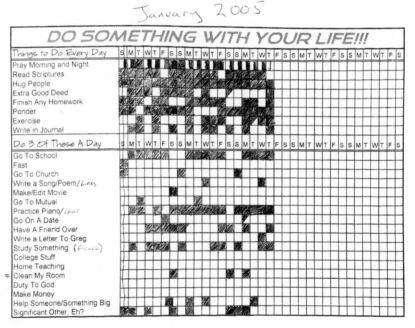

I actually created an Excel spreadsheet for my life. Apparently I hugged people a lot.

EXPRESS YOURSELF

"Wherever God has put you, that is your vocation. It is not what we do but how much love we put into it."

—Mother Theresa

Life isn't, and won't ever be, full of doing whatever you want. You will always have something you have to do. Even if you get the perfect job where work always feels like play and you never want to leave the office, you still have to wait in line at the store. Or you have to talk to someone who is difficult. Or your car breaks down on the very day you didn't want it to. Or your private jet is in great shape but the pilot is sick.

Not to mention, like everything else I talk about in this book, life is happening today. We're not going to wait around for some perfect situation before we can be happy, which means we should figure out how to be happy today. So here's a solution.

Put love into it! Apply your style to everything you do, and you will be doing it with love.

I've had many jobs over the years. My first job was at Subway. My job title was Sandwich Artist. That was to make me feel like I was doing more than *just* making sandwiches; I was making art! It was a very deceiving title, because my boss got really mad at me when I actually tried to make art with the sandwiches. If you imagined a guy boss, you might be sexist. Tammi was a hardcore lady who wasn't taking any nonsense from a teenager pointing out the inconsistencies of the job description. We parted ways, congenially, and I was officially a working man with real job experience under my belt.

I moved on to other jobs. I worked at a movie theater with my friends from high school. Actually, Matt didn't get hired, but everyone else did. We made sure to make fun of him a lot for not being smart enough to work at a theater.

I worked at a factory making magnets with a bunch of Russian brothers. So in case you were wondering, that's the reason I got into Russian techno.

Living our best life, without Matt

I did summer sales, concessions for BYU sports, instructional design at BYUIS, engineering and programming jobs over the summers, and three different research positions.

Every chance I could, I put my spin on it to make the job more interesting. One summer I worked at a software company. The product was simulation software, where you build a 3D factory, from the machines and assembly lines to the moving parts, pieces, and people involved. There was a lot to it, so my job was to help customers figure out ways to set up the software to simulate exactly what they wanted. Problem solving is always interesting, but I can't say every minute of this job was thrilling. Then I discovered that you could set up a simulation, fly around the 3D world, and record it while it was running. You could also make the objects move however you wanted to. So I applied my style and made my job more interesting.

I made the people in the simulation carry boxes back and forth to the beat of Flo Rida's "Good Feeling." Then when the beat drops, the boxes start changing colors and the machines jump up and down. Eventually boxes are flying in the air, and everything in the factory is dancing. It sounds like a huge waste of time.

I showed my boss, and he thought it was unique and fun. In fact, he liked it enough to put it in the marketing materials. They were showing my ridiculous video at trade shows and expos, and all because I was too bored to keep doing things the conventional way. It used to be on my YouTube channel, where you could watch it, but they took it down for copyright infringement of the song I used.

Do what you can to make the things you have to do more interesting. I'll admit it isn't always easy. When I did summer sales for Living Scriptures, I met someone who owned a video graphics company. I told them I was interested in that stuff, and they said I could stop by. I ended up doing an internship with them while I was supposed to be selling. So I ran out of money and went back to Provo, where I worked until school started again. You can make anything more interesting. Except sales.

DON'T QUIT YOUR DAY JOB

This isn't a book about blindly following your dreams. If you quit your job, and you blame me for it, I am going to run away screaming.

You have to be a responsible person. If you need your job to pay your bills, then keep your job. If you want to do something else, find time to do it while you still have a job to support you. If you can't find time, then you are probably in one of two situations. One, you are already filling your time with something that is important to you, so why do you need to do more stuff? Or two, you are filling your time with stuff that isn't important to you, so why are you doing it?

I'm not pretending that every situation is simple. But if nothing else, we can fall back on things we have already talked about. Be grateful for what you have.

However, there may come a time when you can make a leap, and it's different for everyone. I'm very conservative. Leaps of faith are important, but there should be some evidence that your faith is in something real. Don't just fly off the handle and call it a leap of faith.

Even Jesus didn't jump off a cliff when Satan told him to. Oh also, don't listen to Satan.

Every step forward requires faith. I waited until I had a job offer at Studio C, and even then it took faith to take that job, because it wasn't as steady and secure as my engineering job. It meant that if I went back to engineering, I would be behind. It meant that after Studio C was over, I would have to figure out the next step. It took faith to do it. You have to be willing to make a leap, but do it at your own pace.

If you get too hasty, you can get stuck in a trap. A trap is anything that is easy to enter and hard to escape. It is easy to quit your job. It is easy to drop everything and drive to LA. It is easy to leave your kids at home alone and travel the world, but don't justify it by saying, "It's okay, I orphaned them, because they will become Batmans." That's not a leap of faith; that's an escape plan. You're running away from something, and it's a trap. Because once you think running away is a viable option, it's hard to get rid of that mindset, and even harder to deal with the consequences.

So maybe the test for whether you are making a leap of faith is this. Is it easy now and will it be hard later? Then maybe it's a trap. Is it hard now, and are you okay with it being hard as long as it takes? Then that might be a real leap of faith, based on your willingness to do what it takes to make it work, and letting God fill in the rest.

IT'S NOT WHAT YOU HAVE BUT WHAT YOU DO WITH WHAT YOU HAVE, SO DO WHAT YOU HAVE TO DO

"Long only for what you have."
—Andre Gide, French author

This quote from Andre Gide is a beautifully simple way of expressing the idea that you should never seek to have more. What you have changes all the time, and you have no control over whether you have it or how long it lasts. Focus more on what you *do* than what you *have*, because no one can take away your choice to do things genuinely and live fully.

Long to know yourself better and bring out the potential you aren't using or haven't used in a while. If you want only what you have, the only thing to do is use what you have in a better way. When you aren't wasting effort getting more, you make the most of what you already have. In the context of finding yourself, it makes you dig deeper into the one thing you always have, which is you. Isn't that the sweetest?

I didn't start doing sketch comedy to make money. When we were in Divine Comedy, we weren't making any money. We did it for the love of it, and honestly, parts of it were more enjoyable at that time.

I think nostalgia is so strong because it's remembering not just what happened to us but also who we were in that moment. We remember parts of us we love, parts of us we pity, and the growth we've experienced since that moment. We feel nostalgia because we are able to look back and love ourselves more from the future than we could at the time. If you long for who you already are, you get to enjoy who you are now instead of waiting for nostalgia.

Now it's time for the seventy-year-old man in me to come out and yell at you. Stop wanting more followers on Instagram! Your Instagram experience literally doesn't change at all when someone follows you. The pictures you see depend on the people you follow, so the only reason you want people to follow you is to say you have more followers. People I don't know ask me to follow them on Instagram. Why would I do that? I don't know you. You aren't posting anything special for my sake, and I would have no context for your cat pictures.

Listen. I totally get it, because it would be cool if someone famous saw your page and all that, but it is so unimportant. How long can that last? I'm not perfect. I have an Instagram, and I am yelling at myself as well, because I also worry too much about how many likes and comments and followers I have. I start to wonder, when I see that I lost some followers, what it is I'm doing so wrong. It's just a ridiculous thing to think. Maybe if I were using it to sell stuff, that would affect my business or something, but other than that it's just vanity.

Being materialistic isn't the only way to let having more become too important. It can be having more recognition. It can be having more people like you. The funny thing about that is the best way to make friends is to be a really good friend. Long for the friends and family you already have. Really take the time to care for and love them, and you won't want for more friends. And yet, more friends will come. People need good friends, and if you can truly be a good friend to people, that alone will give you a joy you can't find with any possession or any number of followers.

DON'T ASSUME THERE'S ONE ANSWER

This one is pretty self-explanatory. No one's life has one trajectory, and you can have many purposes in life. I may have worked really hard to get an engineering degree, but that was no reason to not take advantage of a unique opportunity to be a comedian. Until then, I did some good work as an engineer, and may go back to that work if it becomes the best opportunity for me. So don't think you have just one purpose! You have many talents that can be used to better the world in a multitude of ways; just keep your eyes open for the opportunities. You aren't wasting time, or killing puppies, as long as you are being true to yourself and putting your heart into what you're doing.

Do you like Toy Story? Ed Catmull, the president of Pixar, had one goal in life. He wanted to create a film that was one hundred percent computer-animated. Toy Story took many years, had many ups and downs, and was close to completely failing. Finally, the movie was released and it was a huge success. Suddenly, he had no idea what he was doing. Pixar had a great future because of Toy Story's success, but Catmull felt lost. He had already fulfilled his goal to make the first computer-animated feature. He explains this experience in his book, *Creativity Inc.*

> It wasn't that I thought Pixar had "arrived"—or that my work was done. I knew there were major obstacles in front of us. The company was growing quickly, with lots of shareholders to please, and we were racing to put two new films into production. There was, in short, plenty to occupy my working hours. But my internal sense of purpose—the thing that had led me to sleep on the floor of the computer lab in graduate school just to get more hours on the mainframe, that kept me awake at night, as a kid, solving puzzles in my head, that fueled my every workday—had gone missing. I'd spent two decades building a train and laying its track. Now, the thought of merely driving it struck me as a far less interesting task. *Was making one film after another enough to engage me?* I wondered. What would be my organizing principle now?[9]

If you read the book, you find out he did find new purpose. How did he find it? He basically wasted time. He observed the people around him and thought about how he could help them in the process. Since he wasn't driven by his purpose anymore, he helped others who were motivated by their own purposes. Eventually he found that his purpose was to help form and maintain a culture at Pixar that would create the best environment for people. Toy Story was a huge success, but on a personal level, it was a nightmare for a lot of people, working one-hundred-hour weeks and not seeing their families. People would be so exhausted they would sleep at work for days without going home. By just being observant and listening to people, Catmull found a new purpose, and the culture at Pixar to this day makes it one of the most desirable places to work in entertainment.

I had a plan for my future as I was getting ready to finish college. Two times actually, I had a job lined up, and then it fell through. The first was the summer before my last year of school. I had been working with a professor on some research, and he had connections at MIT that were going to give me a research position out there. That was my dream school, and I had a professor saying it was almost certain that I would be able to work with his old team over the summer. It didn't work out. They didn't have the funding or something. So, a few weeks before summer came, I suddenly didn't have any plans, and I had turned down another internship in anticipation for MIT. But then Studio C started that summer. I was able to be in the original cast of the show because my internship didn't work out.

Cut to a year later, and I was promised a job doing aeronautical engineering. I planned all year to prepare for that job, even looking at places in Boston my wife and I could live. Sure enough, it didn't work out. Apparently, even though I was qualified in every other way, I had to have a master's degree to fill the position. I told them I was working with the team lead over there, and they said they were sorry, but the computer wouldn't let them finish the paperwork unless they could click the button that said I had a master's degree. There was just no button for me.

Again, I was a couple weeks from school ending, but this time I was graduating. After two months, I found a local engineering job at CSimSoft, about twenty-five minutes away. Meanwhile, Studio C continued, and since I was local I was able to stay on it. Soon after, the show became big enough that they hired the cast full-time, and that became my job. I would never be where I am today if I insisted on the one career path I had in mind. If you're lucky, life won't go according to plan.

There isn't one singular thing you are supposed to be. You don't have to wait around to find your one true calling before you are extremely valuable to the world. You don't have to spend years mastering one perfect role before you feel like you're fulfilling your purpose. If you do, you may still find yourself like Ed Catmull: once that purpose is realized, you feel lost and purposeless. Then you have to find a new one. Luckily for him and for all of us, we have the potential for many purposes as long as we are unequivocally, audaciously, and relentlessly genuine.

There is no other option. You answer to only one person: yourself. But since yourself is overflowing with untapped potential, it's hard to avoid the sin of defining yourself by your roles. Instead, you should define yourself by your style, and then apply that style to whatever role you happen to be in. The difference is, you may have little control over what role you play, but you have total control over *how* you play that role. You will lose yourself if you define yourself by something you have no control over.

For example, if you define yourself as a "Beloved High School Math Teacher at the Best School in the District," what happens when you get fired? Suddenly, you have no purpose because someone else changed your role? That's silly. And if you're thinking, *Jokes on you, James! I have tenure! I'm invincible! (maniacal laugh),* what if a student tells you you're the worst teacher they've ever had? So much for beloved! (Non-maniacal laugh, because I feel really bad when students say that to teachers. Teachers get paid way less than they should and they work hard, you little punks.) Or what if there is a family emergency that requires you to relocate, or a personal emergency that hinders your ability to teach, or your doppelgänger frames you for murder?! It could happen!

Alternatively, you could define yourself by your style: you love teaching, you love math, and you love encouraging people. Getting fired has no effect on your purpose. If you're not teaching at a job, you're teaching your kids how to ride a bike. If you're not doing math in the classroom, maybe you have your hobby of programming computer games. If you're not encouraging students, maybe you participate at church, where you have a knack for helping people to apply their faith in difficult times. Obviously, these are only a few examples of how to use your style to live with purpose. I hope as you read these examples, you came up with your own. This works for any of the situations above, especially the last one: You use your skills to prove in court that it was mathematically impossible for you to have murdered the victim by pushing over a vending machine, because you're too weak to exert the necessary force! Hey, if there is ever a time to admit your weakness, it's when it will keep you out of prison.

These are very simple examples. In reality, you could fill a book with the many ways to apply your style to the roles you play. In fact, the point of this sure-to-sell-a-million-copies book is to help you spend your life doing so.

Here are some oversimplified examples from my own life:

- I was not born to be a comedian; I was born to be funny.
- I was not born to be an engineer; I was born to think analytically.
- I was not born to be a father; I was born to love, serve, and make silly faces.
- I *was* born to be an Olympian, but . . . you know, you make your choices.

So let's assume you've found your style. A very simple example might be you love theater, woodworking, and robotics. Now what? Do you build high-tech movie sets? Is that your purpose? Will you build robots that are beautifully designed and perform on stage? Is that your purpose? What we've learned is you could be happy doing any of these combinations of inspirations, but which one is the most productive and helpful to the world? That's where we come to Section 3: Stop, Collaborate, and Listen.

Most of our purposes in life are not found in isolation. When we think of living with purpose, we often have other people in mind. We want to make the world a better place. The only way to do that is to get out there and work with the world. Just like Ed Catmull, we will find greater purpose as we work with people and apply our style to their needs. As we listen to others and learn their needs, we will be inspired by what we have learned about ourselves to bless their lives in a way no one else can.

Here is a list of things you can try to expand your experience to find your style:

- Take a class, in person or online.
- Go on a hike.
- Eat weird stuff.

- When you have a question, force yourself to come up with ten more questions about that same thing.
- Try different ways to exercise, or invent new ways.
- Watch a movie and do what one of the characters does.
- Try to move objects with your mind.
- Read books from a genre you have never read.
- Learn a different language.
- Learn your own language.
- Do something upside-down.
- Give more than you are asked, and then keep giving.
- Try to do the thing you told someone else they did poorly, and find out how hard it is to do things well.
- Get lost on Wikipedia. Look something up, then click links in that article, and keeping clicking through links and discovering new things.
- Meditate.
- Notice the next time you have the thought, "I can't do that." Try doing it.
- Ask someone about what he or she does, and listen.
- Find a charity to give to, and see what interests you the most.
- Google "life questions" and answer them. I don't know what will come up, but it will probably be interesting.
- Go a whole day without talking.
- Destroy this book in a creative way.

NOTES

1. Richard LaGravenese, dir. *P.S. I Love You*, Warner Bros. Pictures, 2007.
2. Deepak Chopra, *The Seven Spiritual Laws of Success: A Practical Guide to the Fulfillment of Your Dreams* (Amber-Allen Publishing and New World Library: 1994).
3. Jane Nelsen, *Positive Discipline* (New York: Ballantine Books, 2006).
4. Julian Treasure, "5 Ways to Listen Better," presented July 2011 at TEDGlobal, TED video, 0:12, https://www.ted.com/talks/julian_treasure_5_ways_to_listen_better#t-2435.
5. Ibid., 3:18.

6. Austin Kleon, *Steal Like an Artist: 10 Things Nobody Told You About Being Creative* (New York: Workman Publishing Company, Inc., 2012).

7. Elizabeth Gilbert, *Big Magic* (New York: Riverhead Books, 2015).

8. Martin Short, *I Must Say: My Life As a Humble Comedy Legend* (New York: HarperCollins Publishers, 2014).

9. Ed Catmull, *Creativity, Inc.: Overcoming the Unseen Forces That Stand in the Way of True Inspiration* (New York: Random House, 2014).

Tip 3:
Stop, Collaborate,
and Listen

col·lab·or·ate
/kə-ˈla-bə-ˌrāt/

verb

1. See the greatness in people, be inspired by them, and work with them to find a better life than you could on your own.
2. Breed collies and labradors together, and work with them to find a better life than you could on your own.
3. Be nice.

Origin
"Ice Ice Baby" by Vanilla Ice

Example
"'Use *collaborate* in a sentence,' said the teacher."

synonyms: Cooperate, participate, Ice is back with my brand new invention, Something grabs a hold of me tightly, then I flow like a harpoon daily and nightly, will it ever stop? Yo I don't know, turn off the lights and I'll glow,[1] etc.

Most people have sung "Down by the Bay" at some point in their childhood. But most people have *not* sung "Down by the Bay" for three straight hours at a cabin in their adult life.

We went up Provo Canyon with some friends to hang out at a cabin. It's a beautiful cabin with an open family room and kitchen area. In the back, you cross a bridge up to a fire pit. Eventually, we all ended up at the fire pit chatting. Jenny Gray started talking about how she loved to sing "Down by the Bay" with her family, so naturally we all made fun of her. As part of making fun of her, we started singing the song in mockery to show her how childish it was.

We got so caught up in making fun of Jenny that we sang for over three hours. I have never sung any song for that long. We had about thirteen people, and each person would come up with something in succession until we got back around to the first person, at which time we would switch themes. We did a *Lord of the Rings* theme, superheroes, *Harry Potter* theme (twice), and a few others. Have you ever seen a Snape, eating a grape, down by the bay?

It's surprising what great things can happen if you just let it. As embarrassing as it sounds, it was one of the most fun nights I can remember.

This section is about looking outside of yourself and letting your environment guide you in a big way. They may be the lyrics of Grammy-nominated hip-hop sensation "Ice Ice Baby" by Vanilla Ice, but they are also the perfect words to describe the process you will learn here. *Stop* trying to do everything on your own, and stop trying to do it perfectly. You find your style not so you can be amazing and rule the world, but so you can do amazing things with others to make the world better. *Collaborate* with others and your environment. Adapt to the situation and people given to you instead of stubbornly doing things your way, because you never have the only right answer. *Listen* to others and your environment. Don't assume you know everything about how to do something or what the problem even is. You can fritter away so much time and energy going in the wrong direction just because you didn't take the time to listen.

Before you can collaborate and listen to other people, you have to believe they are worth listening to. Just like you had to believe in yourself before you could find your style, you have to believe in others before you can find your collective style.

EVERYTHING IS AWESOME

People are great, and this simple fact is so easy to forget. When we're caught up in our selfish day-to-day activities, we tend to treat people like inconveniences. We expect them to do things the way we think is right or get out of our way.

We consider the cashier at the store an inconvenience the instant they take longer than we wanted on something and we start to get frustrated. We consider the person driving in the next car an inconvenience when we get angry with them for merging in front of us. We consider our kids inconveniences when they don't do what we say and our first impulse is to get frustrated. We planned our day to go a certain way and these people are ruining it!

Open your eyes to the greatness in people. Look at them for just a second and recognize it. You open up a world of awesomeness when you see people's greatness. You will see their inherent goodness, and you will want to work with them. You will see their potential and you will want to learn from them. You would want someone to do that for you, so start by doing it for others. Be the change and all that.

My four-month-old daughter is amazing to me. She learns new things every day. When I want to get something done, I completely forget that and get frustrated when she won't stay still for two seconds so I can put her pajamas on. When I take the time to see her greatness, suddenly and naturally I will start talking to her more lovingly. I'll notice her discovering things, and the crazy thing is, she will calm down. It's like she can sense what I'm feeling toward her. Well, she will calm down a little bit; it's not a complete transformation, but it is amazing. I'll notice that she is reaching for something, and if I can let her touch it or hold it, she might even stay still the rest of the time.

It seems like a small thing, maybe because my daughter is a small thing, but it can have a huge impact on people. You see their inherent goodness, and you both feel it. Imagine if we took a few seconds to notice the greatness in others, especially as they are frustrating us. If we stop thinking of ourselves and take a step back, we can see that they are trying to do what they think is right. They are caught up in the same selfish cycle that we have been caught up in all day, and they are just trying to move forward with their efforts to make life a little better. Sure, they may be doing it wrong, but so are we, so stop taking it personally.

When I was in sixth grade, I took a few seconds to see the greatness in someone, and it completely turned an enemy into a friend.

We were at recess playing two-hand-touch football, because no one wants to deal with a bunch of kids damaging each other. My team was killing it, and one of the kids on the other team was unhappy about that. I don't remember his name, so we'll call him Stuart. Stuart was a rough kid, and he wasn't afraid to get in your face if he didn't like you. Well, he didn't like me. I don't think he ever liked me, because he loved to be mean to me. He especially didn't like me when I took the football out of his hands and scored a touchdown. It was really unfair too, because I never did sports things correctly, so I wanted to enjoy this rare moment.

He pushed me a little and I told him to calm down. Everyone told him to calm down as well, and of course he got even madder at me for the embarrassment of a bunch of people telling him to calm down. As we started walking back to class, he pulled a cheap shot and tackled me from behind. It was a full-on pile driver, and my face went right into the ground.

It hurt, of course, but it's not like I wasn't used to that kind of pain due to my brief but memorable foray into the wide world of swing set–diving comedy I told you about earlier. But my face got a little bloody and dirty, and there was no shortage of witnesses, which was to my advantage. I had every opportunity to finally get this punk in trouble.

For some reason, I decided not to. I don't know if it was because of a Sunday school lesson I just had or something, but I had compassion on the little guy. I looked at him and realized he was terrified but trying to hide it.

Turns out, I didn't even have to tell the teacher. Everyone else had already told him by the time I got back to the classroom, plus he saw my face. He took us both outside of the room to figure out what happened, and I said we were just playing around and I fell. When Stuart realized I was trying to not get him in trouble, his face completely changed. The teacher asked him if I was telling the truth, and he just nodded. Looking back on it, the teacher must have known I was lying, but he also probably knew the kid didn't have many friends.

Everything with Stuart changed after that. Instead of picking on me all the time, he defended me in every situation. He would give me Snack Packs. He was like my new bodyguard. It didn't transform the kid completely. He was still a bit of a punk, but a punk that was on my side, so he wouldn't let people mess with me. Not many people messed with me after that—not because he was a good bodyguard, but because he was the only one that was messing with me before.

Stuart had goodness in him, and it wouldn't have done anything other than make a bigger enemy if I had decided to retaliate. When I saw his inherent goodness instead of just the negative stuff he was hiding behind, he changed surprisingly quickly.

No matter what people are doing with their potential, that potential is in them. One of the beautiful things about being part of the interconnected human family is that we have the power to bring it out of them. Will you choose to see people for their shallow exterior? Or will you bring out the goodness in people that you know is always waiting to be brought out?

YOU CARE! I CARE!
WE ALL CARE FOR ICE CARE!

"The problem with the world is that we draw the circle of our family too small."

—Mother Theresa

When I was in Italy, I experienced this observation from Mother Theresa in a tough way. Italians are very strongly loyal to family and very strongly skeptical of anyone else. I was a missionary walking around looking very American in my white shirt and tie and unfitted slacks. When I would try to talk to people, their first question was often "Do I know you?" They didn't care to talk to me if I wasn't in their circle. They would often wave me off and say, "I don't care. I don't know you." It was tough to hear all day. After a while I got so used to it that I would just say something like, "We're all in God's family," or "Maybe we knew each other in the pre-existence." Sometimes they would be intrigued and I would have a great conversation with them. Other times they would say I was trying to trick them and tell me to go away.

I also experienced the opposite. Once they consider you family, they treat you well. One time there was this Italian lady who was pretty cold toward me until I won her over by mentioning, of all things, a tomato. It didn't matter that we were part of the same church. It didn't matter that when she invited us to her home for dinner (out of a feeling of obligation, I'm sure) that I complimented her home and gave a spiritual message to her family. What mattered was when she served us salad, and I ate the tomatoes in it, I guessed what type of tomato it was.

This was no small feat, mind you. I was pretty proud of myself for being able to recognize the type of tomato—of which there are many—by the taste and texture.

She just lit up when I mentioned it. She could not believe an American would be so attentive to her culture and care enough to know how to distinguish a tomato. From that day on, she was all about us. She invited us to dinner far more often than she had invited missionaries before. She made sure to say hi to us every Sunday. All because I showed the smallest inkling of caring about something she cared about.

We can make a huge difference in people's lives just by caring about them, and it makes a huge difference in our lives as well.

Sometimes we think that showing we care has to be some grand gesture. We often fail to follow through because it feels so unnatural. It shouldn't be that hard, and it really isn't. All it takes is to be genuinely intrigued by people, which will happen automatically when you look for their greatness.

So, what does caring about people have to do with finding your purpose in life? Part of my goal for this book is for you to have a goal to apply your style to make the world a better place, but you can't make the world better if you don't care about it. Or maybe caring about people is your purpose. That's a great purpose to have, when you can find your style and your niche and go to work doing good in a way that only you can do. My closest friends have come out of caring about people ahead of caring about results. And again, the results ended up better as well. When I was in Divine Comedy, I had no idea how important my relationships with my cast mates would become.

When I first got into Divine Comedy, all I knew about these people was that they were funny and I wanted them to like me. I presented my very first sketch, "Dead Wedding," and it went well. It got to my head real fast, and I thought I was pretty great. It went well in front of an audience and made it into the "Best Of" show. It's embarrassing to admit, but I thought I had some pretty great ideas of how to make the shows better. I was just an excited kid who had something go well, but I was about to be humbled.

My hat is backward. That means I'm cool.

That sketch was probably the highlight of that year for me. I did get a few other sketches in that year, but they didn't go as well, and I soon realized I had a lot to learn. I was also humbled by my wife's comments on ways to have better stage presence. Apparently, I moved around too much and used my hands very weirdly when I tried to be expressive. I was further humbled when I played a part where I was supposed to be the "hot guy" and I thought I was nailing it, but then the club advisor said, "This character isn't supposed to be nerdy. He's supposed to be cool." Ouch.

I was humbled, but I still wanted to do everything I could to make the group better. I had good intentions, but the problem was that I thought the group needed to be better in the first place. I had way too much ambition. I literally presented the idea of turning our auditions into a mock American Idol thing, where, instead of an audition with a one-day callback, it would be a six-week process where we film it and post it on YouTube and use the audience to vote people off until we get the final people who would stay in the group. *This was a college group!* Ain't nobody got time for that!

My friends were very considerate for listening to my idea. But instead of that whole mess, we just added a show the night of callbacks so we would have a chance to work with people before we brought them into the group. The goal was to find people that were good to work with, because the number one cause of bad things happening in the group was when people were hard to work with. Adding the show was a great way to get us closer to that goal. It didn't matter that my original idea was terrible. It showed that I cared, and that led to good results.

We've always said the magic of the group was how much we cared about each other and how much we cared about what we were doing. When we were on the same page, and we cared about making each other look good on stage, the feeling was palpable, even to the audience. Divine Comedy was on a high, selling out every show within hours, and it was all because we made each other a priority. We certainly weren't the most talented people on campus, but we might have been the group that most believed in each other's talents. Again, it wasn't perfect, but caring doesn't have to be perfect, it just has to be what you want the most.

One of the most magical times of Divine Comedy for me was our acting workshop trip to New York. School was out, no work to go to, just a week of doing what I love with a group of people that loved the same thing. This is when I found out Matt always travels with a towel, and he doesn't sleep in a bed.

When we got to our hotel, the room for Matt, Jason, and me was not available for that first night. We had to walk across New York City to stay at a different hotel last minute. It was a fun forty-minute walk, but when we got to the hotel, we found out we were supposed to bring the purchasing card with us. It was about 12:30 at night, but it didn't stop us from being able to buy street kebabs on our forty-minute walk back to the first hotel. New York City is amazing like that.

So we got the purchasing card and made the walk again. Around 2 a.m. we finally got our room. The only room left was a single king bed. We were so tired we didn't care, and even Matt slept on it. It was a strange bonding moment, but the best ones always are.

The trip was amazing, and at the end we were all exhausted. We immediately started to crash when the trip was over, so we all slept on the floor of the airport.

How many of these people can you name?

Divine Comedy was the closest thing I would get to a fraternity at a college that doesn't do fraternities. It was more than something to do; it was connecting with people who had the same interests and forming lifelong friendships.

I think it's super important to maintain those relationships. This is something my wife has taught me, because she has always stayed in touch with close friends. She has friends from high school that keep in touch from states apart, and when they get together they pick up right where they left off. Relationships are important, and it's always worth the effort to make them last forever.

We can't just assume someone knows that we care about them. In fact, we can't just assume we actually *do* care about someone. We may know in our minds that we want the best for someone, but do our actions actually show that? And if we believe our actions show that, is it shown in a way that they can understand?

In *7 Habits for Highly Effective People*, Stephen R. Covey talks about the emotional trust bank account. If our account is full, we can mess up a little and it won't be a big deal. But if our account is low, even little things can set the other person on edge. If you feel like you're walking on eggshells with someone, it is your responsibility to fill that emotional bank account up.[2]

The way you fill it up is by doing things *they need* to gain your trust. Notice I didn't say you could do any good thing for them. It has to be something that builds trust in *their* eyes. You have to speak their language. If you love receiving chocolate, and it makes you feel loved by the people who give it to you, that doesn't mean giving chocolate to others will make them feel loved. Maybe the person you want to gain trust with feels loved when someone walks his or her dog. So what you should do is walk their dog, even if it would mean nothing to you. This is a very basic summary of the "love languages" concept. You can read that book if you want to know more. My love language is getting chocolate in the mail, just so you know.

The more you withdraw from a bank account, the more you need to deposit to compensate. It is the same with your relationships. The more you interact with someone, the more transactions you have, either positive or negative. People who are in your life every day give you a lot of daily support, so you need to make sure you are giving a lot back.

This explains why people who live with each other can get annoyed with each other more often. I have a certain way of doing things, and I want certain things done, but the person I'm living with has their own agenda as well. We are bound to get in each other's way. Let's say my wife really likes her pickles cold, but I tend to leave them out, because it makes no difference to me. At first, she just puts them away. But every time I leave the pickles out, I make a little withdrawal from my wife's trust account. It starts to add up, day after day, as she walks in on a lukewarm jar of pickles, until eventually she feels like I must hate her if I'm so inconsiderate that I'm willing to subject her to tepid pickles. Now I'm really in a pickle, because my trust account is so low that the next time I do anything inconsiderate, she will get upset.

I leave a hammer on the kitchen table.

"Are you kidding me?!" she asks, understandably upset.

"What?" I respond, with surprise and a bit of fear, because I don't understand why she's upset.

"Why is this hammer on the table?"

"Because I hung up a picture for you. Sorry, I thought you would want me to do that," I say, with sass.

Now *I'm* feeling like she doesn't care, because I think my service is so generous and charitable and I'm the nicest husband ever and how could she not be ecstatic that I hung up a picture.

"Just don't leave the hammer out."

"Right, because all I do is leave things out and I never do anything nice for you," I say, indicating the super nice thing I did.

"That's not what I said. Stop being so sensitive. And YOU'RE NOT ALLOWED TO HAVE PICKLES!"

"YOU CAN'T KEEP PICKLES FROM ME!" I yell as I run out the door crying.

If I had a nickel for every time I ended an argument with that phrase.

If you live with someone, even if you love and appreciate them as deeply as I love and appreciate my wife, you've probably had experiences like this. If you work with someone, you've probably had similar feelings, even if they've never escalated into a verbal argument. Life is about relationships, and we have to fill our trust accounts when they are low. It is always worth it.

Is there something you do that the other person brings up often? Are you sick of them "nagging" you about it? Try this. Ask them to let you know any time you do that thing wrong. Show them you want to listen. You will make a huge deposit of trust the next time they say something and you *thank* them, and then *react positively*. Do not make excuses! Don't even ask clarifying questions! Just say something like "Thank you, I will do better." If they're real hardcore about their criticism, or you have a long history with this particular thing, they may not believe you right away. That's okay. Because every time you make that deposit, even if you have a large deficit to make up for, you will slowly gain trust with them. I can't promise you'll change them completely, but if you are patient it will lead to a better situation.

Give more than you take. Make it a point of pride to see how much you can give without taking. In the bank account analogy, it's like earning more than you spend. It's a comforting and satisfying feeling to see your bank account grow and grow because you are being frugal. You will have the same feeling with your relationships. People will love being around you, because they feel love coming from you.

But James, what if no one does the same for me?

They don't have to. The magic of this is that when you give to others, you are giving to yourself. It's an investment, and you get the interest. It's a win-win situation. Of course, don't stretch yourself too thin. You always have to go at your own pace. You're only human. Unless you're a cyborg, in which case you might also consider your battery levels.

Think about where you got what you have in the first place. Whatever you have was given to you. Whether you believe it's God or nature, you got what you have from someone or something else. If you don't give to others, you are stopping goodness from flowing. When you do give to others, you cause goodness to flow through you, from where it came to where you send it. It's that flow that makes us happy, not the taking. So if you want flow, just start giving, and the universe will give and give through you.

Rich people aren't happy. Generous people are happy, no matter how much wealth they have to give.

Popular people aren't happy. Friendly people are happy, no matter their social status.

Powerful people aren't happy. Charitable people are happy, no matter their abilities or influence.

Just like anything else we talk about in this book, if it is real, it is in your control, and it takes practice to get good at it. Leo Rosten, humorist and political scientist, said, "It is the weak that are cruel. . . . Gentleness can only be expected from the strong."[3]

Whether it's a relationship with others or your relationship with yourself, it's all about giving. Invest some trust in your friends, family, and even coworkers and acquaintances. It's amazing how much love you get when you give it away.

THE OL' GRIND

At some point in your life, you have to get a job. It's probably what was on your mind when you decided to read this book. I've gotten all touchy-feely, and you're wondering what all this has to do with getting the best job you can and being happy doing it.

Hopefully you see the connection to everything I've talked about. Finding your style helps you determine what you might want to do in your job or how you want to put your spin on any job you do. Seeing the greatness in someone makes you interested in what you could do with or for that person. Caring about people makes you better to work with and inspires you to give your heart to what you do.

This chapter is my two cents on how your job fits into it. Your job isn't everything, but you will definitely spend a lot of time at a job, so it's helpful to know how to get a good one.

A dream job is not all about the money. If that were the case, more people would be happy and fulfilled with jobs that just pay well. But I'm pretty sure that everyone's real dream job is to do whatever they feel like doing that day and then get paid whatever they feel like getting paid. And that is more of a fantasy than Albert Camus in rubber ducky footy pajamas riding bareback on a bear's back while it rides a unicycle. So what's the solution then? What makes a dream job a dream? You guessed it, being genuine and applying your style. The more genuine you are, the more you will grab opportunities that make your job enjoyable and fulfilling.

My dad told me a story about when his brother was a radio DJ. This was in the seventies, when the coolest thing in the world was radio, and being a DJ on the radio was the greatest job ever. He spent a day at his brother's work and had a great time. Afterward, my dad said he was so jealous and wished he could have a job like that. My uncle said something that surprised my dad. He told him that sometimes his job was fun, but any time he wished he were somewhere else, the job became drudgery.

Even the best job requires you stick to something when you would rather be doing something else. Right now, I'm editing this book, which I'm super grateful to be doing, and I can't wait to see it published. But right now, I also want to finish building the bookshelves I've been working on for weeks, and I would love to be outside with my wife and daughter playing in the kiddie pool, but I have to get this done. And my ADD is kicking me in the pants right now.

It's okay that the instant you don't feel like doing your job, no matter what the job is, it will partly be drudgery. Any time you would rather be doing something else, your job won't be the most enjoyable thing in that moment. That is what you should expect. You aren't looking for perfect bliss at all times, just something you can look back on at the end of the day and be proud you did *something* that mattered to you. At the end of today, I will be *so* glad I stuck to it and stayed on schedule for finishing this book.

A job is not a dream, because you are expecting someone to pay you. No one is going to pay you to do what you want to do. They pay you to do what *they* want you to do. If you happen to want to do what they want, then lucky you! But that won't always be the case.

You don't choose how to make money based on what you feel like doing; you choose how to make money by the opportunities presented to you by other people. You can paint all day long, but if no one needs a painting, don't expect anyone to pay you for it. The same goes with boring stuff. You shouldn't get paid just because you're bored. You can mow lawns all day long, but if no one actually wants their lawn mowed, they aren't going to pay you to do it. And you might get arrested for trespassing.

Can you imagine if the world worked like that? You hear someone at your door and you open it to someone singing.

"Hey there, I was a music major and I graduated with honors. My rate for singing is $600 an hour, and I've been singing for ten minutes."

"That's a crazy high rate!"

"I'm really good, though."

Dang it, now I have to give this guy a hundred dollars because he wanted to sing to me.

You spend a lot of your life at your job, so it makes sense that you want your job to have purpose. But there's nothing wrong with your job's only purpose being to fund the rest of your purposeful life. You can be happy at your job, doing work you would never choose to do otherwise, because you find purpose in feeding your family, or saving up for charity, or using that money for any purpose that matters to you. Some jobs are like that, and some jobs are more inherently purposeful. Life is long, and you never know how jobs will change. You can come home from your not-so-exciting job to live your dream life as you play with your kids and weave blankets for homeless people on the weekends.

Here's my best advice on how to get hired. Don't try to convince someone you are the best person for the job; just convince them that you will make their life easier.

Have you ever had a salesman convince you to buy something because it was the best in the world? You probably don't care to buy it.

You either don't believe the person is telling the truth about it being the best, or you don't care about some random product just because it's the best. For example, if someone wants to sell me the best glue gun in the world, I don't care to buy it because I don't need a glue gun. If you are a normal person, you have never bought the best car in the world. You went for a car that had what you needed. You went for a car that solved your problem of getting from A to B and had the few features you cared about. If you're unlucky, maybe the salesman suckered you into buying upgrades, but if you don't actually care about those upgrades, you regret buying it. The last thing you want is for your boss to regret hiring you.

You need to solve their problem. In some ways, this is inherent in the hiring process, because they list what you will have to do. So you come in saying you will be able to do those things, but so does every other applicant. How do you set yourself apart? Your boss just wants their life to be easier. If they didn't need another person to solve their problems, they wouldn't go through the hassle of hiring someone. Therefore, your goal should be to solve their problems and make their life easier. Most candidates make the interview about them; you will make it about the person hiring you.

If you had a previous job, instead of listing the duties you performed, talk about how you made you last boss's life easier. Maybe they had a hard time teaching an employee, and you came in and helped train that employee. If the person you want to work for hears that, they will think you will do the same for them. That tells them that whatever the circumstance, regardless of the tasks you were assigned, you're creative enough to make your boss's job easier without them having to tell you every little thing to do. If they hire you, they can trust that you'll come up with solutions on your own, and nothing is easier than that. They would be crazy not to hire you.

The great thing about this is, for all of you who have never had a job before, you can use any example from life!

"I made my mom's job easier by volunteering to play with my brother when she was stressed. If you hire me, I'll come up with ways to take your stress away."

"I made my teacher's job easier by collecting the students' homework and handing it to her. If you hire me, I'll be proactive in getting people organized."

It doesn't matter how big or small it is, you are showing your aptitude for creative problem solving.

This might go without saying, but money doesn't buy happiness. We all know this, but we still think we want more money. It's very hard for me to not want more money, and my excuse is that it means more security for my family. While that is partially true, I also want more money so I spend it on things that temporarily make my life easier.

No matter how much money you have, you will adapt to it and think you need more. If you have enough to survive and get your basic needs met, you can be as happy as anyone.

Monetary success does not always mean that you are "blessed." Nor are you somehow more righteous when you do have wealth. A lack of wealth does not mean that God doesn't love you or that you've done something wrong. My advice is not to mix those two things up. You should always be grateful for what you have, but don't equate your amount of wealth to your level of righteousness, or you'll get all sorts of messed up spiritually if and when things go down.

If you're not sure where your priorities lie, here's a good question to ask. Would you rather be poor in a happy relationship or rich in a broken relationship? No one would admit out loud that they would choose to be rich in a broken relationship, but they will ask for days if they can have both. No, you can't have both. That's not how "Would You Rather?" works. It's also not how life works. One is a priority over the other, even if they are your top two priorities. When a choice comes where your relationship and your money are at odds, what are you willing to give up? I can honestly admit that there have been times where I was scared to be poor in a happy relationship. It's not easy, but do whatever you can to make money a servant to your life and not the other way around.

It goes back to prioritizing the things that don't change—the things that can't be taken away from you. All your money can be taken from you. No matter how much you have, you can regret not having more. The creator of Victoria's Secret was doing great financially, and he sold his company within five years for about a million dollars. That sounds like plenty of money to me. However, two years later, Victoria's Secret was making billions of dollars, and he committed suicide. It's a super sad example of how you can always think you don't have enough.

I won't pretend that I don't worry about money sometimes. But I am more at peace with my situation now. I'm in a happy relationship and that makes me feel pretty rich. And earlier tonight, my eight-month-old daughter crawled on top of me laughing. I was so happy when I thought she wanted to give me a kiss, but she was really just trying to eat my face, which, I think, looking back on it, makes me even happier.

WE ONLY LIVE TO SERVE

Nothing will make you happier than serving people. We are social creatures, and we are meant to be together and help each other. If you want a dream life, make a dream life for someone else.

Use your style to bless everyone's life. You may think you're only blessing *someone's* life, but that goodness spreads beyond what you could ever know.

There is no better satisfaction than knowing you made a difference in a way that no one else could. You may think your contribution isn't unique, or that someone else would have done it anyway, but I don't believe that's true. If someone else wanted to be helpful, they are welcome to be helpful. You aren't stopping them by doing what you can to help. You are just adding to the good being done, and no one would ever say there can be too much good done in this world. So even if someone else would have done the same thing, they will probably still do service somewhere else, and now you doubled the good in that situation. There's no limit on giving love.

This chapter is exciting for me, because there is no better application of finding your style. No matter what you do in your life, if you switch your mindset to service, every action you take, even the most menial tasks, can become meaningful.

CAN SERVICE BE WASTED?

You should never regret doing something that you believe is good for someone else. It doesn't matter how much they appreciate it. It's similar to the mindset that nothing is of value unless you get paid for it, which of course is not true. Someone's appreciation for you is like social currency. It feels good, but it is only temporary.

Whether they show appreciation doesn't change the fact that you created good in the world in a way that you believe is good. If they don't appreciate it enough, you may not get the benefit of that social currency, the energy that comes from someone else's positive energy, but you shouldn't regret it. You still improved life; you created positive energy. Whether or not they bounce it back is another story. You may need to get energy from other sources, and you may decide that means you have to serve that particular person in that particular way less, so you have room to get that energy back from elsewhere. It can get exhausting to do something for someone that they never appreciate, but never doubt that the good has been done and karma dictates that the positive energy will get back to you somehow.

Being a dad has taught me the importance of not waiting for someone to appreciate you. If I worried about how much my infant daughter appreciated how hard I work to provide for her needs, I would go crazy. No matter how many times I explain it to her, she never thanks me.

I do everything I do because I love her, and I believe that what I am doing is important. It's important for her to grow and feel loved and be taken care of. When I do things for her, I get all the joy a person can get from serving someone even though she's a thankless little ingrate.

To be fair, I am richly rewarded when she smiles at me. My little heart aches every time I hear her laugh. I see her learning things, and it's more entertaining and uplifting than any show and more fun than any game. It's just the best.

We do, however, need to be recharged.

We can't just keep giving and giving nonstop. We have to receive in order to give: to receive rest in order to give energy, to receive inspiration in order to inspire. These are the raw materials we receive and form into meaningful and unique gifts for others that no one else could have given. You're transforming what you receive into what you give.

Someone who is good at giving has to be good at receiving as well. You have to care about what you receive so you can care about the gift you turn it into. I'm talking about gratitude for what you have, but I'm also talking about being more aware of what you have. The simple act of seeing potential in what you already have can recharge your mind and make you want to give. One of the most satisfying things is to make something out of what seemed like nothing.

Instead of wanting a different situation, try caring about what you already have. If you hate your job, it might be because you don't care about the resources and tasks given to you, so you don't care about what comes out of you. You have no emotional or spiritual relationship with it. You just drink your Red Bull and get through the day. Instead of being genuine, you ignore your style, shut off your mind and spirit, and robotically let your body transform Red Bull into busy work.

I've seen happy people in almost every job. It's not because they have the one job they can be happy in; it's because they are true to themselves and take ownership of what they are doing. They get joy out of their own personal interpretation of what's great about their situation. What if you decided to care, even if you didn't think you could? Like when I rocked out to Cobra Starship while meticulously cleaning the Jamba Juice I worked at with my friend Justin. Or like when my high school friends and I sang a cappella songs to people at the movie theater as we handed them popcorn. Hey, your style doesn't have to be the same as mine.

It's that flow I was talking about earlier. Light bulbs don't work unless they give and receive current, and the more energy that flows through them, the brighter they glow. A battery does nothing, no matter how much energy it has, when it's connected to a broken circuit. The battery eventually just rots. Hoarding what you receive will make you rot too.

Exercise is a great example of flow for your physical body. If you hoard the nutrients you put in, you store fat, get slow, and die. If you use those nutrients to do work, you get strong. Then you take in more and give more in a virtually endless cycle of buffness.

Just like our other skills, service takes time to get better at, so start practicing now. You still have to give and receive at your own pace, but never stay stagnant, and you will get stronger and stronger.

HOW TO BE A SERVICE SUPERSTAR

MIT did a study on productivity. They put groups of people together to perform certain tasks, and measured how well they did. They discovered three types of groups. The first type of group had one person with a high IQ, a potential superstar of solving problems. Surprisingly, those groups didn't perform very well. The second type of group had a combined high IQ; everyone was more intelligent, so maybe they'd really solve problems. They didn't perform particularly well either. The third type of group, regardless of their IQs, performed the best, because they had *high social sensitivities*. They listened to each other and had greater empathy. This created an environment of synergy that brought out the best in each person. Those groups also had more women in them.[4] Which got me thinking, "Why are there only four women out of twelve cast members in Studio C?" Food for thought.

This study shows us that the point of finding your style is not to become the superstar. Because no matter how good you are at your purpose, you will never be as good as a group of people who works well together. Margaret Heffernan, a business expert, author, and

119

TED speaker, talked to producers of hit albums about their superstars. They said they had plenty of superstars, but they didn't last. The ones with long careers were the collaborators who brought out the best in other people and therefore the best in themselves.[5]

Back in Divine Comedy, when we would hold auditions, we would narrow it down to the funniest few people for callbacks. But once we had about fifteen people we thought were funny, it wasn't about finding the funniest of those fifteen people. The only thing we looked for at that point was who was good to work with. The result of that was creating a group of people that would bring out the best in each other, and that far outweighed the talent of any single person.

I can't tell you how many times this has happened in my marriage. I had an idea of what life would look like, only to find there was something even better that I never would have thought of on my own. Sometimes it was just God's timing, but most times it was just listening to my wife. She took this book from a hodgepodge of random information and helped me to get to the heart of what I was trying to say. You think this book is bad now? You should have seen it before my wife fixed it. I'm most excited about life when my wife and I work as partners to create a future that is beautiful and unique to us.

Working with people is most often the way to a better result and a happier you, and the way to work with people is to serve them. Listen to them first with your social sensitivity. Make sure to recharge by taking a step back and realizing the beauty in what you already have and the potential of the people and things around you. Then add your style to all of this and see how naturally things work out for your good and the good of everyone around you.

WHAT DID YOU EXPECT?

Don't expect anything from anyone. Bold statement? This obviously extends from the idea of taking control of your own happiness. You can't control anyone, so requiring anything of them for your happiness means giving them power over your happiness.

For some reason, my wife hates this concept, while I find it extremely useful for not letting others get me down. I think that's because she thinks I'm saying we should never expect anyone to do anything, which sounds like the same thing. Now that I've said that out loud, I realize I should probably clarify what I mean. I'm lucky to have such a smart wife that checks me on things. Thanks, babe!

If you have no expectations, nothing can get you down, because there's no way to disappoint someone who doesn't expect anything to happen in the first place. If you don't expect someone to be nice, it won't bother you when they aren't nice. If you don't expect someone to help you, it won't bother you when they don't help. We can even go more extreme with it. If you honestly don't expect someone to not rob you, then it won't bother you when they rob you. It might seem extreme, but it makes sense, right? It's not up to you if someone robs you, but it's up to you if they rob your happiness.

Where my wife draws the line is you can't just walk around with zero expectations. You have to expect certain things from people. You have to expect people to be decent, or else people can't get along. You have to expect people to do their jobs, and people that don't should get fired. Students are expected to do assignments and pass tests, or they shouldn't graduate. There should be expectations of people that make the world go 'round and help us have some structure in society, and I agree.

But not when it comes to your happiness.

Setting boundaries, making rules, and following through on consequences are absolutely necessary. But recognizing that no one is perfect and you will constantly run into mistakes is also necessary. Imagine if every mistake (or even purposeful error) had no effect on your happiness. It requires that you have a little faith in the idea that things work out in the end. Maybe it requires a lot of faith, but you will be rewarded for that.

Here are a couple examples. There's no reason why you can't set your expectations for an employee, and then if they have proven themselves ineffective and hopeless, fire them *without getting upset about it*. Yes, the expectation was there *professionally*, but you *personally* don't have to let it upset you.

If you're a teacher and your student can't graduate because he failed the class, you can say, "I did what I could to help you, but I guess you just didn't make it. I'm quite proud of what I've done for you, and I have no regrets." Then walk away, ignoring their pathetic pleas for you to change their grade when they never seemed to care about it when they had the chance.

But let's get back to you. What does this mean for you, day to day? It means that even though people should be *expected to act* a certain way, your happiness is only affected by how you *expect to be treated*.

Has someone done something to upset you recently? Why did it upset you? Chances are, you had some expectation for how that person should behave, and they acted a different way. Instead of focusing on other people's behavior, you should instead focus on yourself and how you think you should be treated.

For example, someone says they don't like you. Why do you get sad? Is it really because they shouldn't act that way? Not really. If that were true, you would get sad every time they acted that way, whether it was toward you or someone else. At any given moment, someone is telling someone somewhere they don't like them, but are you constantly sad? Of course not. You're sad because you feel that *you should be treated* a certain way.

But is that true? Does it really matter that someone says they don't like you? As a person who is on TV, and in the public eye, I can guarantee you there are people that don't like me. Someone just posted a very long poem on my Instagram about how terrible my work is. First, they took the time to write a poem—it rhymed and everything—about how they used to like our show and now it's so terrible we "need to STOP!" Second, I'm pretty sure they reposted it on each individual cast member's Instagram. Freedom of speech and all, but that's pretty intense.

Should I really let it get me down though? It doesn't matter why they did it, and it doesn't matter if they would change their minds if

they just got to know me. The point is, I'm happy anyway. I'm insecure enough that if a close friend were to say it, I would be hurt. I'm
not perfect. But I still think the ideal to strive for is that if a friend said
something mean to me, I wouldn't take it hard. I could even shock
them and say, "That's okay. Anything else?" and maybe they would
open up to me. We might even resolve a real problem that might not
have otherwise been resolved. Worst-case scenario, you learn something, whether about yourself or them or the universe.

Forgiveness is one of my favorite things. I don't mean other people
forgiving me; I mean the freedom and peace of forgiving others.
Forgiveness is the purest manifestation of not expecting people to be
a certain way for you.

I don't understand why people speak about forgiveness in terms
of it being a service to others or being about what the other person
deserves. Forgiving someone makes *your* life better, not theirs. Do you
think they are the one affected by your negative feelings? Or is it you
that is really trapped by bitterness or antagonism? If someone does you
wrong, and you hold onto it for years, while they go off and live their
life, it is you who suffers for it.

I started learning what forgiveness really means when I learned
Italian. The word isn't that different, but the way it is presented in the
language indicates a gift being given. The word is *perdono*, and it is
made up of the words *per* and *dono,* which mean "for" and "gift."

What this made me realize is that forgiveness is turning something into a gift. When someone does wrong to you, they essentially
steal something. Whether they literally steal something, or they steal
your comfort with pain, or they steal your dignity with shame, or they
steal your peace with threat, they are stealing something good you
had. When someone steals from you, you are missing something that
belongs to you, and that person owes you a debt. There is a hole there
that will remain until it is filled. By forgiving someone, you are essentially saying, "This thing you stole is no longer stolen. I am turning
it into a gift. I am deciding to let go of that thing and see it as a gift,
turning a negative debt into positive transaction of love."

123

Of course, this does not mean everyone you forgive deserves your trust. They have to fix that part of it. They may never do that, and you may need them out of your life in the worst cases, but your peace and wholeness are completely yours to keep because you have nothing stolen from you. All you have are gifts given to other people, and as we already talked about, giving creates the flow that happiness is made of.

Isn't it a beautiful thought that you have the power to turn the worst of situations into happiness through forgiveness? I'm not saying it's always easy, because bigger offenses are bigger mountains to climb. But the more effort required to create forgiveness, the greater the reward. Give yourself the time needed, but start on the path of forgiveness as soon as possible. It is so worth it.

DON'T WIN ARGUMENTS

My favorite story about an argument with my wife—and we laugh about this often—happened in the first year of our marriage.

I don't remember what the argument was about, but we were definitely still in the first-year-adjustment stage of our marriage, and we were still getting used to living with each other's different styles. We were newlyweds, super excited and deeply in love, but misunderstanding things that would cause confusion and we'd have little fights.

I had done something for her that day, but I had also messed something up. I was arguing that my intentions were good, and she was arguing that I didn't listen and I had broken a promise. As I started to get really emotional, I just wanted to yell out, "I love you, and I just want to do things for you!" But instead, with all the emotion of a husband desperate to connect with his wife, I yelled, "I just want to do things *to* you!"

It immediately broke the tension. We both started laughing like crazy, and we soon forgot what we were fighting about. If you're too young to know why that's funny, don't worry about it; it's like why the chicken crossed the road, same joke, nothing else.

I'm ashamed to admit it, but there are far too few times where I have truly listened to Brenna *from the beginning* of an argument. My tendency is to defend myself, because I want her to know I love her, and therefore, she should never be upset with me ever. If you've been in a relationship, you know it doesn't work that way, because no matter how much you love someone, you can do really annoying things.

One of the moments I look back on where I actually did it right— a moment I try to learn from to this day—happened when we were eighteen. We weren't even dating at the time, because I was a really annoying boyfriend and I couldn't figure out what I wanted. I broke up with Brenna four times before I figured things out. One of those times was our senior year of high school. I may have broken up with her, but I couldn't stand being without her. I know, I'm obnoxious. It's okay, though; she married me anyway.

After high school, I wanted to remain friends with her. I didn't want to be in a "serious" relationship, because I knew I would soon be leaving on a mission for two years. I struggled with defining the relationship. I just knew I wanted to be around her. As you can imagine, it was a few months of trying to figure it out, feelings being hurt, going back and forth on what we really were. I wanted to just be friends, but I wanted to go on casual dates with her. I wanted her to know I loved her, but I didn't want her to expect "boyfriend things" from me. It was as stressful as it sounds.

Meanwhile, my family moved to Idaho. Our relationship got even more complicated, because at this point, the only way for me to talk to her was on the phone. But since I wanted to call her often, it started to feel more serious to be committing so much time to making sure we were talking. Brenna was very understandably having a hard time with it. It was getting to a breaking point where she was confused and feeling like I was dragging her around. She was ready to be done because it was too hard.

I knew I had to do something or I was going to lose her, but I still couldn't commit to being her boyfriend. The answer was to finally listen. Every time we would start talking about our relationship, I would try to get her to realize that I cared about her and that it was better for us to be friends than to never see each other. The more I said I cared about her, the more confusing things would get. I finally realized I needed to listen.

It was the hardest thing I had ever done. I was so tempted to go back to my habit of explaining away my behavior. She would say that I was doing things that I wasn't actually doing, and it was so tough not to tell her what I thought she needed to hear. I wanted to tell her I never said or did or wanted any of those negative things she was saying I did. Instead, I just said, "I'm sorry. I understand why you feel that way. I don't know why I did that." The more I said I was sorry, the more she got upset and asked me why I would do all those things. I was dying to say she made those things up in her head and was making it worse for herself. I didn't do that. I just kept pushing through, apologizing and saying I wanted her to be happy.

She hung up the phone on my hundredth sorry, and I felt like a complete failure. I thought it didn't work. All that effort to listen to her felt like a waste, and I still felt like I should have tried one last time to explain to her why everything was okay the way it was.

I sat in my room, crying and wondering what was going to happen. About fifteen minutes after she hung up, she called me back. I couldn't believe it. I answered the phone, and we had the best conversation we had had in many months. I was able to still have Brenna in my life, even though I was doing so many things imperfectly, because I *showed* her how much I cared about her instead of trying to *convince* her I cared.

Obviously, this was a very personal example of listening to people and not trying to win arguments, but the same goes for any relationship, personal or professional.

Daniel Cohen, a philosophy professor, gave a TED Talk called "For Argument's Sake."[6] He argues that arguments should be positive experiences, not negative ones. We make them negative by making it a competition. But who really wins in an argument? If you were the one who learned something, we refer to it as losing an argument, because you weren't right. Daniel Cohen calls this the war model. In reality, the person who learns something wins. The other person didn't gain any knowledge. At best, they may have had the pleasure of teaching, if the argument was amiable. At worst, they got a temporary ego boost.

Losing or winning an argument depends on what you end up with afterward. If you leave the argument frustrated, angry, or hungry, then you lost. If you leave educated, uplifted, or with pizza, then you definitely won. Arguments can and should be win-win, unless you're on the debate team. In which case, you turned talking into a competitive sport, and we've already established that I'm terrible at sports, and how dare you.

This is great news! You never have to win an argument again! If you're as bad as me at winning arguments, you don't have to worry about it anymore.

But James, what about the situation where I really want something to happen, and I need to win an argument to make it happen?

You really don't need to win any argument over the other person. How often have you changed someone's mind by winning an argument? It doesn't usually happen. In fact, in *7 Habits*, Stephen R. Covey talks extensively about how you should "seek first to understand, then seek to be understood."[7] People lose clients, sales, friends, and family because they tried their hardest to convince the other person of their opinion. Over and over again, when people sought to understand the other person first, they saved their situation as well as developed a better relationship with the other person.

You may have said a hundred times, "If I had a camera and I could show you, I would prove to you I'm right." Guess what? Even if you could, it wouldn't make a difference. That's not a bad thing. It should give you hope. Again, it proves there is no point in winning an argument, because the person needs to be listened to, not educated. Don't shout why they are wrong. Ask why they feel wronged. Recognize that these feelings they have are real, because they are only trying to get you to address those feelings. Say you're sorry even if you aren't at fault, because the word sorry also means you feel bad.

I hope this chapter does give you hope. I hope you can feel free to talk to people, for the sake of making things better rather than trying to be right. Go up to someone and say, "I want to lose an argument with you." And just see what happens. That's not real advice, but if you do it, please film it and send it to me. That seems like it would be hilarious.

THE LAST CHAPTER OF THIS SECTION

It's time to bring people together and make things happen!

If you are thinking about your Confidence Triangle, trying to become genuine, brave, and humble (or weird, stupid, and wrong), this part of collaborating requires bravery. In other words, bringing people together requires you to feel a little stupid because you have to be vulnerable and strong and the same time.

You use your style in the relationships, jobs, and communities you are already a part of. Now it's time to take the next step. It doesn't have to be overwhelming. Don't take the next hundred steps at once. Just take the next step and be a better team player.

I love the feeling of being on a good team. I may be terrible at sports, but I'm a great teammate! In my six weeks of being on the volleyball team in my sophomore year, I was the most supportive teammate those people had ever seen. I was cheering everyone on and telling them how good they were doing. They didn't often say the same to me, but that's only because it wouldn't have been true.

I would actually take water bottles and bang them against the bench to get cheers going. I was shameless, but even if it was a little strange, it made the team a little more upbeat. Or maybe that's how it went in my head, and I was really just annoying, but it's not my fault they didn't openly communicate that to me if that was the case. To be fair, they didn't have my Oscar-winning book to help them realize that.

Being on the team was fun, but I didn't feel like I belonged. I guess it wasn't my style. When you have more fun cheering than you do on the court, you're probably a hardcore theater nerd and should be okay with not being on a sports team. Being in a choir and being in plays gave me enough experience being on a team and in situations where I could actually contribute positively. You can't perform songs unless your choir team is in harmony. Pun intended. And you can't perform plays unless your team . . . does the play together. Pun missing.

In *Creativity Inc.*, specifically on page 74, the page I smudged chocolate on, Ed Catmull talks about the team at Pixar being the reason for the company's success. "If you give a good idea to a mediocre team, they will screw it up. If you give a mediocre idea to a brilliant team, they will either fix it or throw it away and come up with something better."[8] *Toy Story 2* was a good movie in its own right and not "just a sequel," because of the great team that worked on it.

On page 75, the page my daughter crumpled, Catmull says, "Ideas, though, are not singular. They are forged through tens of thousands of decisions, often made by dozens of people."[9] You don't get some genius idea and work on making it a reality. You get great people together to solve a problem, and you get to be surprised by the result. So much insight, and that's just pages 74 and 75! I can't wait to read the first 73 pages! What, you don't always start books on page 74? Don't knock it till you try it.

Tanya Menon, an organizational psychologist, says the secret to great opportunities is to widen your social circle. Everyone, at some point, is in a situation where things don't go their way. The difference between more and less successful people is successful people *grow* their network and start looking outside their circle, while less successful people tend to retreat, because it's the more comfortable thing to do.[10]

Being uncomfortable is always necessary for growth. Exercise hurts, studying hurts, and being a better person hurts, because it's a law of nature. The same applies to your ability to reach outside of your circle.

I came upon a really interesting social experiment on YouTube done by Jia Jiang. He decided he would get over his fear of rejection by being rejected for a hundred days. He made up things to ask people where he expected to be rejected, and would consider it a failure if he didn't get rejected.[11] It's pretty fascinating.

He learned a few lessons that made him bolder and expanded his ability to make things happen, instead of being stopped by fear. For instance, sometimes you just have to ask. He went into a Krispy Kreme and asked them to make a donut in the shape of the Olympic rings. To his surprise, the manager took the challenge and did it for him.

Another thing he learned was that instead of running away from rejection, we should ask why. Sometimes the person will have a good reason, but sometimes they will realize there is no reason, and it opens them up to the idea.

The last one that I really liked was that you should express what other people think to gain their trust. He asked a manager at Starbuck's if he could be their greeter, which isn't a thing. The guy thought he was weird, until he said, "Is that a weird thing to ask?" This made the guy realize that it wasn't a weirdo wanting something from him, it was a normal person wanting to do something new and exciting (if not weird). Then they are now as curious as you are to do it.

An obstacle I had to overcome to work with people was this nagging thought: If someone else gets there before me, I will lose my chance.

This is a terrible attitude to have, because it turns everything into a competition. Everyone is your enemy, when everyone should be your ally. The problem in my thinking was that I assumed resources were limited. I wanted a piece of the pie, and if I didn't fight for it, someone else would get it.

My life changed when I learned that I could just make the pie bigger. Instead of fearing that I was going to lose my piece, I knew I had the power to create a bigger pie for everyone, including myself. You can lose one opportunity and still have infinitely more.

This saves you from jealousy, because you can be happy for people if you don't think they are automatically stealing from you. It saves you from being hard to work with, because you invite people to be smarter than you, and you love that people can contribute what you cannot. It saves you from burnout, because you don't try to hoard all the glory for yourself by doing everything without any help.

As you go forward in your lifelong pursuit to find your style, make sure you to enjoy the moments along the way. Make sure you enjoy the people you are working with. Stop thinking that you have to have all the answers when you work with people. Go into a situation freely, willing to learn from everyone. Every day you can wake up excited to collaborate with the people and situations around you because you let solutions naturally find you. Just listen to people, truly care about others and your work, and lose as many arguments as possible. You get to let life surprise you with good things.

Isn't that neat?

NOTES

1. Vanilla Ice, "Ice Ice Baby," *Hooked*, Ichiban Records, 1990.
2. Stephen R. Covey, *The 7 Habits of Highly Effective People: Powerful Lessons in Personal Change* (New York: Free Press, 2004).
3. Leo Rosten, *Captain Newman, M. D.* (HarperCollins, 1961), 32.
4. Anita Williams Woolley, Christopher F. Chabris, Alex Pentland, Nada Hashmi, and Thomas W. Malone, "Evidence for a Collective Intelligence Factor in the Performance of Human Groups," *Science* 330, no. 6004 (October 2010): 686–8.
5. Margaret Heffernan, "Forget the Pecking Order at Work," presented May 2015 at TEDWomen, TED video, https://www.ted.com/talks/margaret _heffernan_why_it_s_time_to_forget_the_pecking_order_at_work.
6. Daniel H. Cohen, "For Argument's Sake," presented February 2013 at TEDxColbyCollege, https://www.ted.com/talks/daniel_h_cohen_for _argument_s_sake.
7. Covey, *The 7 Habits*.
8. Ed Catmull, *Creativity, Inc.: Overcoming the Unseen Forces That Stand in the Way of True Inspiration* (New York: Random House, 2014), 74.
9. Catmull, *Creativity, Inc.*, 75.
10. Tanya Menon, "The Secret to Great Opportunities? The Person You Haven't Met Yet," presented March 2017 at TEDxOhioStateUniversity, TED video, https://www.ted.com/talks/tanya_menon_the_secret_to _great_opportunities_the_person_you_haven_t_met_yet.
11. Jia Jiang, YouTube videos, https://www.youtube.com/channel/UCs_ Z7b5JBH1jk4wKOiQHKUg.

Tip 4:
Play Hard, Play Hard

Play·Hard
　　/pleɪ hard/
verb

1.　You know that common phrase, "Play medium"? This is stronger.
2.　Like "work hard," but you see life as a game.

Origin
OLD ENGLISH: plegian (to exercise), plega (brisk movement), MIDDLE DUTCH: pleien (leap for joy, dance)

Example
"I can't believe the *actual* origin of the word *play* works so well for the phrase *play hard*."

antonyms:	Take yourself really seriously, freak out when things don't go your way, blame others, quit when things get hard, take it personally when someone tries to merge into your lane and make it difficult for them even though we're all just trying to get where we're going so can everyone just calm down.

This is my favorite joke:

What's the difference between roast beef and pea soup?

Answer:
Anyone can roast beef.

Get it?

I love it because it always takes people a moment to get it.

This section is about changing the way you look at hard things. There are ways of looking at things that have completely changed my life for the better, and I want them to change your life too. When you make that switch in perspective, you'll get more than a laugh; you'll live your dream life.

This section comes last because it's kind of the "endure to the end" part. You've read about respecting yourself, finding your style, and working with people, so now you have the skills. I mean, you have everything I could think of in the timeframe of writing this book. Play Hard, Play Hard is a play on the motto Work Hard, Play Hard, which was my family's motto growing up. Most of the time the motto really meant Spend the Morning Weeding, and Then We'll Go Bowling. I changed it to fit the new paradigm of Life Is a Game. We don't need to separate work and play, because every work we do is just another challenge in the game of life.

When I was a kid, I was obsessed with the idea of mind over matter. I may have failed every night I tried to be Matilda (that's right, Matilda. Not Luke Skywalker, Matilda), but eventually I learned what was real about mind over matter and what wasn't.

I did this thing where I would pretend the shower wasn't cold. I would turn on the cold water and say to myself, "The water is warm. The water is warm." I would go in and the water would be cold. *But* I would shiver less, and I would get used to the temperature. I guess it was more like I was ignoring the temperature, so it didn't affect me, and I was able to take a full cold shower. It wasn't because I didn't have access to hot water; I was just a weird kid.

It taught me something really cool though. Even when I can't change my circumstances, I can use my mind to eliminate the power of bad things over me. In this case, I actually could have changed my circumstances, and yet I preferred the challenge of getting by with less. This was one of my first encounters with seeing life as a game, and it got me excited to do the same with other challenges in my life.

When I was first living on my own, my parents helped pay for my food. I would try to get by with less. I think they gave me about $50 per week. One week I got by on $10, and I felt pretty good about myself. When I was in high school, every once in a while I would try to talk as little as possible for a whole day. It was often motivated by being my overbearing self and feeling self-conscious that people were sick of me talking. It made me notice more when people would talk to me and had the added bonus that I felt like people even missed me. It was like a fast from talking—a talking cleanse, if you will.

A lot of good has come from looking at things differently, and all because I decided to change my perspective. This change in perspective is often referred to as a paradigm shift, and the first chapter in this section is dedicated to explaining that paradigm shifts aren't nearly as boring as they sound.

IF AT FIRST YOU DON'T SUCCEED, MEH

The dream life is not a destination. There is no place to get to. That's one of the hardest things to get out of your head—this idea that there is a time in the future when everything pays off and you can feel at peace, a time in the future when you've "made it" in life. You can feel the joy of it just by thinking about it. You imagine in your mind's eye a confident and accomplished you. Nothing is more confidence-building than the feeling that you've made it. But imagine if you figured out a way to feel like you've made it *today*. That's what a paradigm shift can do.

The most likely situation is that you won't get to an ideal spot where all your dreams have been realized. If you're like me, you don't even know exactly what that looks like, other than you have everything you need and you can do whatever you need to do to be happy.

But what about the case where you do make it? Even if you know exactly what it would take to "make it," and your entire aim is to get there, what happens when you do? This is like the Ed Catmull situation after *Toy Story* was made. He had made it, and it didn't fill him with celestial peace and leave him flying unicorns in bliss for the rest of his life. All it meant was he had no idea what to do next. There is no situation in which you've made it in life and have nothing else to worry about.[1]

The good news is this dream situation in which you have everything you need and you can do whatever you need to do is possible right now. It doesn't mean everything you want, because no one has ever gotten that. It means everything necessary to love your life. There's nothing in particular you need to have before you can build your dream paradigm.

Stephen R. Covey compares paradigms to maps. He gives an example of trying to find your way to a location in Chicago, but the map of Detroit was accidentally printed.[2] With the wrong perception of your terrain, you get frustrated and want to give up. Even if you double your efforts or your speed, you still won't get where you want to go. A paradigm is simply the way you look at things, and a good paradigm will steer your behavior to the desired outcome.

Don't misunderstand me. I'm not talking about magic or lying to yourself or pretending something is real when it's not. I can't suddenly be a cool person just by shouting it at people, because apparently, according to that guy I just yelled at, that's not what cool people do. I'm talking about turning on the light in a dark room to see what is actually there. A map doesn't change the reality of the situation; it only serves as a tool to understand reality. The better the map, the more likely you'll get where you want to go.

I have been told my whole life, in a million ways, *what to do*, but it hasn't always been valuable for personal growth. Only in times when I've been taught *how to see things* has my life really changed for the better, and the change lasts longer. But we still won't change anything if we don't act on that new way of seeing. This combination, of seeing things as they really are and then changing behavior to match that, is the power of the lessons I've learned.

My life is a dream, not because I pretend it's a dream, but because I've put the required effort into building a dream based on good paradigms. You don't get buff in one day of working out, and you don't get paradigm-buff in one day either. But you do get adrenaline and a feeling of satisfaction from day one, in both cases.

I definitely have moments where I don't *feel* like my life is a dream, because I'm still working on strengthening my paradigms. But because I'm on the right path, I always *know* deep down that my life is a dream. I have this constant, underlying peace that everything will be okay. In fact, that everything will be incredible, because the Latin root means "unbelievable," and I can't believe how amazing life is.

Nothing in my life is perfect, and it never will be. I've gotten to the point where I don't even want it to be perfect. I would be bored. I love the struggle, the fear, the pain, the failure, and nothing can keep me down for long. What's the main attribute of a boring game? No challenge! What's the attribute of a boring life? No challenge! Let's stop making excuses for our negativity.

If you ever find yourself thinking, "I still need one more thing and I'll be totally happy," or "I still can't live a dream life because of [insert thing you can't control here]." Know there's a paradigm somewhere that can change your mind. I do the same thing, so my advice is to not give up. I've learned to accept that there are a million things that could change in my life to make it different in a good way, but that doesn't mean it would make it better. The grass is always greener on the other side, but it won't make you any happier than your own grass.

Grass is also literally greener on the other side, because of your vantage point. If you are looking straight down at your own lawn, you can see between the blades of grass at the dirt and abandoned army men and all that stuff. But when you look out, you're seeing the grass at an angle so all you can see are the blades. You see more green, hence the grass over there looks greener.

The point is, if you want greener grass, look at it from a different perspective. Also, fertilize and aerate. People forget how important that is.

That being said, don't forget to dream. After all, a dream life can't be built without dream bricks. And you'll need some dream windows, and dream furniture. Don't forget proper dream heating and dream air-conditioning. My only regret with mine is not installing a dream waterslide that goes from my dream bedroom straight down to my dream pool. Oh well, next time.

My point isn't that you should never want more than you have; part of dreaming is thinking about wonderful goals you can set for your life. My point is you should never *need* more than you have. You should be happy whether or not your goals come to fruition. You should be happy even when things get taken away from you. Even while mourning those things, you should have inner peace.

Usually, life has better plans than you thought up, if you're willing to be open to what life has to give. Think of a spoiled rich kid. Everyone knows what a nightmare that kid is. But you'll also notice, that kid is never happy either. He isn't throwing a tantrum because he's happy that he gets what he wants all the time. He's throwing a tantrum because getting what you want too often leads to selfish entitlement, and it can never be gratified.

Don't think you are any different from that kid. He didn't plan to be spoiled, but he has this idea that he needs everything to go according to his own plan. The idea that something won't go his way causes panic. We can look from the outside and think, "Calm down. People are trying to do what is best for you." But he will never feel that way unless he's open to accepting that he doesn't know everything. If you're lucky, things won't go according to plan.

YOU HAVE SPECIAL MIND POWERS

Henry David Thoreau, the indisputable baller of transcendentalism, said, "I know of no other fact than man's ability to elevate himself with thinking."[3] We have the power to elevate ourselves with nothing other than what's in our heads. No other tools needed.

I saw this chart that showed the chances of success for every attitude you can have toward something. It started with "I won't," giving you 0 percent chance of success. Then "I can't" gives you 10 percent.

"I don't know how" gives you 20 percent. It goes on through every 10 percent increase until "I am" gives you 90 percent, and "I did" gives you 100 percent.

I love that their process for being 100 percent successful in life is to just say you already did it.

Mom: Go clean your room!

Me: I did!

Boom. Cleaned

Or if you have lofty goals in life:

Me: I want to be a doctor. No. I can be a doctor. No! I did!

Boom. Doctor

That's not really how the power of the mind works. You don't just change things like Matilda (not Dr. Strange, Matilda) by just thinking about changing or moving them.

However, and this is a big however, I do think we can change external situations through the power of the mind. It's a hard thing to talk about, because on one extreme we have moving objects with your mind, which seems impossible, and on the other hand we have simply changing your attitude, which is completely within our control. Somewhere between those there is a line we cross where we can influence external things.

For instance, we can influence someone by asking them to do something. No, we don't have control over them, but it can have an influence on their behavior without us exerting any physical force. Sometimes we don't even have to say anything. I can detect when my wife is sad, and it changes my behavior. My dog can detect it. Some argue that even our plants can detect changes in our moods, but if that's true, my cherry tomatoes are jerks because they've squirted juice in my eye on the worst of days. Not helpful.

So how much influence can we really have with our thoughts? Jim Carrey uses the law of attraction in his life to become successful. He once wrote himself a ten million dollar check for "acting services rendered" and dated it three years from that day. He kept it in his pocket, and three years later he made ten million dollars. He talks a lot about intention.[4] Nothing is done, or ever has been done, until someone had the intention to do it. You don't sit there thinking, "When is it going to come?" You have to think, "It's already here."

His father was an example to him of what can happen when you let fear disguise itself as practicality. He did the practical thing and got a job as an accountant, even though he didn't want to. When Jim Carrey was twelve years old, his dad was let go from that job, and the family had to do whatever it took to survive. Jim said, "You can fail at what you don't want, so you might as well take a chance on doing what you love."[5]

In the *Seven Spiritual Laws of Success,* Deepak Chopra explains that there are unchanging laws of the universe that will bring us success if we abide by them. He introduces the book by saying, "When this knowledge [of the laws of success] is incorporated into your consciousness, it will give you the ability to create unlimited wealth with effortless ease, and to experience success in every endeavor."[6]

Wow, Deepak, that's quite a promise. If you understand his definition for success and wealth, though, it actually seems possible. Success and wealth have much more to do with having what you personally need than they do with what everyone says you need. A lot of successful people talk about the law of attraction, this idea that whatever you believe is what comes to you, whether positive or negative. All I can say for sure is that it has worked for me, and Deepak's seemingly improbable statement has been true for my life.

It has been different for me than it was for Jim Carrey, and it will be different for you too. It's one of the many parts of finding your style. You have your unique relationship with God, and you figure out what works for you. I never wrote a check for ten million dollars, because it has never felt genuine for me to do so. That's not how I send my intention into the universe. My style has usually been in the form of believing I can do anything and knowing God loves me.

I always wanted to give a TED Talk, and I believed I had something to say, so I prepared for it long before I ever had the chance to give one. I didn't sit in my room and pretend to give TED Talks, though that might be someone else's style. I didn't imagine the audience complimenting me for such a great talk, as some others have done. My style was to see something that made me happy, and figure out who I would have to become to be ready for that opportunity, believing I could become that.

I knew I could be good enough to be in Divine Comedy. I knew that if I ever got in, I would be able to contribute, but that doesn't mean I knew I would get in the group. I auditioned for plays and even a singing group, because I wanted to be prepared for the time when the right audition came. I auditioned for Divine Comedy three times, and didn't get in until I became the kind of person I would want to work with.

It doesn't even have to turn out like I planned. In fact, when it doesn't, it's always better than my plan. I always just assumed I would marry someone in my faith, so you can imagine my surprise when I fell in love with a Catholic girl in high school. She was incredible. This may seem funny to some of you, but I am a firm believer in my faith, and part of that is marrying someone of the same faith. If you want to know why, feel free to email me, but for the purposes of this book it's sufficient to say I didn't think it would be possible to end up with her. I had a hard time with God because of that, asking why he would let me fall in love with someone I couldn't be with. When I told my mom I was dating Brenna, she asked why I couldn't just be friends with her. I tried that and it didn't work. We were off and on all of senior year because I broke up with her three times, but I couldn't stop thinking about her. All I could do was continue to be true to myself and be patient.

After high school, we went our separate ways but stayed in touch. I went to Italy for two years on a mission, and a few weeks before coming home, I found out she had become interested in my church because she had run into missionaries while going to San Diego State University. Long story short, she chose to follow that faith and became a member of the Church. Suddenly I felt like God had been guiding me all along, knowing this would be someone that I would marry for eternity. She is incredible, and I'm so glad I just patiently followed my heart and let things happen in a way I didn't expect.

Like every other principle in this book, this applies to every part of life: relationships, personal growth, work, etc. Find your way of throwing your intention out into the universe, and be patient with the result. As Jim Carrey describes it, "Letting the universe know what you want, and working toward it, while *letting go of how it comes to pass.*"[7] You can't control everything that happens, but you can ask for things and the desire will find a way around your opposition to get to you.

Jesus said it best in His Sermon on the Mount, "Ask, and it shall be given you; seek, and ye shall find; knock, and it shall be opened unto you." Opportunity doesn't come knocking; you do.

YOU IS SMART. YOU IS KIND. YOU IS IMPORTANT.

Don't believe the myth that intelligence is fixed. Alfred Binet, the inventor of the IQ test, would be appalled at how we use the IQ test to determine people's intelligence. His original goal was to examine the differences in intellect between children *to learn how to improve their intelligence.* He disagreed with philosophers of the time who asserted that intelligence is fixed. In *Modern Ideas about Children* he argued that "with practice, training, and above all, method" we could "increase our attention, our memory, our judgment and literally to become more intelligent than we were before."[8]

This power of the mind stuff isn't just for calling the universe to do your bidding while you binge *The Office* for the seventh time. You can actually increase your intelligence, and become a greater tool for good. I would add that the more you want to use your desire to produce good, the more power you have to bring it to pass.

Start with a growth mindset, and everything else will follow. There is a great book called *Mindset: The New Psychology of Success,* where Carol Dweck gives example after example of people who were successful because they had the mindset that they would grow.[9] Wherever they started didn't matter, because they knew they could grow, and that would always lead to growth.

Affirmations are an interesting way to develop better habits. A good affirmation is five things: personal, present tense, positive, emotional, and visual. Create the affirmation, then spend a few minutes visualizing it in great detail, down to the chair you're sitting in. I didn't realize until recently that my desires were really affirmations. My daydreaming (which was personal, present tense, positive, emotional, and visual) would eventually lead me to take the path to the opportunities I dreamed about.

Isn't basically every movie about how the main character needs to believe in themselves to be victorious? Some are more obvious than others. Spoiler alert: *Kung Fu Panda* is about how the secret to being a true warrior is being yourself. *Penelope* is about how the only way to not be ugly is to love yourself for who you are. *Bambi* is about terrifying children. I hated watching that movie as a kid. From the creepy drip-drop song at the beginning, to the possessed owl spinning its neck, to the frantic murder of Bambi's mother, that movie was so unpleasant to watch that I don't think I've ever watched the whole thing. Anyway, back to the power of perspective. When you have the right perspective, work becomes play, stressful becomes challenging, and failure becomes the best education you can get.

SUBPAR WARS VI: RETURN OF THE CONFIDENCE TRIANGLE

Don't get stuck! You won't always feel like the most confident person, throwing intention into the universe left and right and having everyone praise you as you walk by. It's like when I went to rescue someone from an evil mastermind, and as I was running down the long platform to safety I was shot at by large, sticky cannonballs that stuck to me and dragged me down until the weight was too much and I couldn't move. Or like in the movie *The Incredibles,* when Mr. Incredible loses confidence.[10]

Remember the Confidence Triangle doesn't mean you have beaten all unpleasant emotions about your abilities. It's the willingness to look stupid, weird, and wrong so you can have the benefits of being brave, genuine, and humble. Susan David, a Harvard medical school psychologist (so you can't argue with anything she says) said, "Tough emotions are part of our contract with life . . . discomfort is the price of admission to a meaningful life."[11]

She talks about how we need to be open to all emotions, good and bad. Our emotions allow us to react to our world, to care about those reactions, and to decide what we want to do about them. If we were never uncomfortable, we would never be motivated to fix problems. On the other hand, if we experience the same emotions over and over, it strengthens our resolve to do something about them. It works in us, day after day, so that when we have the spark of inspiration come to fix that problem, we are prepared with the motivation to act on that inspiration.

Without these emotions, we wouldn't be motivated. We could be told the same thing over and over and not do anything about it, but if we are told by our emotions that it is important, then we will do something about it. We can even be inspired with the greatest ideas, world-saving ideas, but if we never experience the emotion that tells us something needs to change, that inspiration will soon fade as we realize it will take work. We fade into thinking maybe things are fine as they are, and what should have become a life-changing effort is reduced to an amazing but dead idea.

It almost seems like we should seek negative emotions. Can that be right? Yes, it can. But remember that it isn't just negative emotions that guide us. Of course, we should be seeking for positive emotions. They are just as powerful to motivate us. There should absolutely be a balance of emotions, because while negative emotions help us to feel deeply what needs fixing, those positive emotions help us understand what needs cherishing.

Just like pain is necessary for working out, it is necessary for emotional and spiritual growth as well. Your perspective is the only difference between enjoying life and being miserable. If you hate working out, all you feel is pain, and you don't see the benefit. But if you understand what you get from working out, suddenly the pain is a sign of good things to come. That pain makes your strength meaningful, because you suffered to get that strength, and that's why it means something to you. Of people that don't want any negative emotion in their life, Susan David said, "You have dead people's goals."[12] The only way to not have discomfort is to die. Obviously, that isn't a great goal.

The problem comes when we think that the only emotions we should allow are the positive ones, so we numb ourselves to the bad ones. Unfortunately, that's not how the brain works. When you numb negative emotions, you also numb the good ones.

When I was in college, I had an experience so emotional that I didn't know how to handle it. My oldest brother, Josh, was hit by a drunk driver and passed away. It was a complete shock, as I imagine all sudden tragedies are. I couldn't even process it. Some days it was hard to fathom that it was real. But while my brain had a hard time dealing with the reality of it, my heart was immediately affected. I went through my day-to-day routine, going to classes, taking tests, going to work, and spending time with my wife. I let my brain and heart fight each other, day after day, with no clue about which one would take over at any moment. I would be deep into an assignment, totally able to distract myself as if nothing was going on. Then the next minute I would be bawling uncontrollably.

My brain would tell me things were the same, my brother wasn't even in the same state, so he must just be somewhere else like he always was. When that drunk driver hit him, Josh was on a bike ride around the United States. He lived in Orange County, California, where he had a recording studio. He was the most talented musician I had met, and he was a great sound engineer. He enjoyed what he was doing, but he wanted to take a break to travel on his bike. He was so happy out there on his bike, camping on the sides of roads, seeing so much of the beautiful country we live in. He saw far more than I have seen, and

I'm sure more than you would notice if you traveled the same roads in a car. He had friends join him for portions of the trip, but other times he rode alone.

He started in California and rode through Utah and down along the southern border of the United States. Then he biked up the east coast, back along the north border, and returned down in California. The last time I saw him was when he passed through Utah. He stayed at our little apartment, sleeping on the couch, and taking a few odd jobs for extra money for his trip. He was able to see me in a Divine Comedy show, and most of my family came down that same week. My brother Anthony was in the Marines out in DC, but I'm sure he was there in spirit. Josh stayed for about a week and continued on his journey.

I remember that he loved New Orleans. It was the perfect place for someone with as much love for music and culture as Josh. I think he stayed there three weeks. He hated Georgia. He said most people there treated him poorly and that southern hospitality is a myth. Cops ticketed him for trying to hitch a ride, because his friend's bike was broken and they needed a ride for 78 miles to the next place with supplies. The cops forced him to walk the entire distance.

The accident happened in South Carolina. He was still with his friend at the time, and they were on a long stretch of road in the morning. It was around 10 a.m. that a drunk driver swerved off the road at the worst time, going far too fast, and hit my brother off his bike. His friend was riding in front of him and didn't even know what happened until the driver behind the drunk driver caught up to him and told him Josh was hit. He spent the next few days in the ICU, and my parents went and stayed with him.

At first, I had no idea he wasn't going to make it. I found out about the accident and I was devastated about his condition, but it seemed like there was a chance he would make it. We would get updates from my parents, and a few were hopeful for a while. He was able to move some fingers, but he never spoke. After almost two weeks in intensive care, he passed away.

I felt more peace than I thought I should. I remember my mom telling us how peaceful she felt. She knew our family was eternal and she would see him again. She was both indescribably sad and totally at peace. That's how I felt, but that feeling of peace was hard to maintain when I had to go back to school and work. Everything felt so pointless. Nothing gave me the kind of joy I would usually feel. Everything that was good was fine. Everything that was bad was fine. I felt so numb and unmotivated. My favorite thing at that time was to cry. When I cried I could feel something. It was a sad feeling, but it was feeling. The worst part of that time was feeling numb. I so much preferred feeling sad to feeling nothing. I couldn't feel fully happy, but I could feel fully sad, so I would go there as often as possible, and that got me through a lot. It also allowed me to come out of sadness in order to feel happiness.

I learned that all feelings, whether positive or negative, are essential to my life. The bright ones contrast the dark ones and make a beautiful painting that would otherwise be only an uninteresting, solid white, which is the same as having no painting at all. That's a

The family that raised me. I love these people like crazy.

metaphor, if you didn't catch that. I'm a terrible painter. That's not a metaphor. I'm an actual bad painter.

MY NAME'S BLURRYFACE, AND I CARE WHAT YOU THINK[13]

One thing I learned from Josh was that you shouldn't care what people think about you, but you should care what people *feel from* you.

I hear a lot of people saying, "I don't care what anyone thinks." The problem with that is you can be inconsiderate or self-destructive, because you think not listening to people is the same thing as being independent or confident. At the same time, worrying too much about what people think can set your brain spinning and cause you to retreat in fear because you don't want anyone to think anything negative about you. But you don't have to worry about caring to much or too little about other people's thoughts if you focus instead on feelings.

No matter how eloquent you are, you can't convince someone you hate that you like them. They will feel it from you. And no matter how clumsy you are with communication, if you really care about someone, it will eventually show. Sure, it takes time, and it's okay if people don't think perfectly of you. How many people do you like that you have had some negative thoughts about? Probably most people. In fact, the more you like someone, the more time you will spend with them, and the more opportunities you will have to run into things that you don't like. So why get offended if people think a few negative things about you? It isn't permanent. If a choir teacher's opinion of me isn't permanent, then nothing is.

One example of a place where it is easy to worry too much about what people think of you is in a job interview. In fact, it is necessary that people think highly of you, or else you won't get the job. But again, focus on how you make them feel, more than proving to them that you are the best candidate for the job. Whatever they may think of you from your résumé or your interview, the most powerful influence over their thoughts about you is their feelings.

One time I had an interview at a company that makes online tools, and I was applying to be a web programmer. I had a couple years of experience in programming, but web programming is different from what I had done. There are, of course, a lot of similarities, but for all intents and purposes, I was significantly underqualified. I showed them a poorly made website that I put together, which I could not have done without tutorials and guide books right next to me, and that was about the closest I got to showing them I was qualified. I may not have gotten the job, but I was pretty proud that I got a second interview.

I mostly just showed genuine interest in these people and their work. I showed them that I worked well with people and that I was able and willing learn. What else do you need? The second interview was with a higher-up in the company. I wouldn't be surprised if the reason he was there was because he was so confused when he saw my résumé and they still wanted a second interview. I must just be *that* charming. In the end, they went with someone else. I guess they preferred "someone who can do the job" over someone who can just come to work and be awesome. Whatevs.

While we're on the topic of job interviews, it helps to be upfront about the fact that you can't guarantee perfection, but you can guarantee that you care.

If you think you need to guarantee perfection in order to be competitive, you're wrong. Maybe you worry that others are saying they are perfect, so they'll go for the other candidates, but that's not true. Everyone can see through that. Everyone knows there is no guarantee of perfection. Which means, if you guarantee perfection, you are actually more likely to turn people off, because they can't trust you. They know you won't be perfect, so they have no idea how qualified you really are. If you are upfront about being imperfect and emphasize your work ethic or passion (but please don't use the word passion if it isn't honestly your passion, because people can see through that too), they will trust you and more likely want to work with you. Tell them you will actively seek to do the best thing, and you will correct your mistakes and get better and better. They want to know you'll proactively figure out how to make up for your imperfections. Speaking to their needs in an honest way is the best way to their heart.

But sometimes it doesn't matter at all what people think of you. If you really like ham sandwiches and someone comes to you and says they don't like that you eat ham sandwiches, you're going to say, "That's weird," and move on with your life, unscathed. Why? Because you have no investment in anyone's thoughts on your choice of sandwich meat. No matter how much that weird person hates ham, you will still get the same amount of enjoyment and nutrition from your sandwich. Your stomach doesn't hear that and go, "Wait a second. Someone just disapproved of this ham. When it comes down, I refuse to digest the ham."

So, where is the balance? In what situations can I wear my black shirt that has "I don't care what you think about me, I don't think about you at all," printed on it? I was an angsty teenager . . . at twenty-seven. The balance comes naturally when you stop thinking about other people's thoughts (which you can never truly know anyway), and just think about what love you can show.

People often say they want to feel normal, but no one really wants to *be* normal. For starters, you'd have to be 50.8 percent female and 49.2 percent male to be exactly average, and no one should feel like they have to live up that standard.

IT'S NOT OVER TILL THE SKINNY, AVERAGE-HEIGHT GUY SINGS

I had an experience in high school that taught me to worry a lot less about what people thought of me.

I was in choir. What?? A theater kid in choir?? How original!

Anyway, I took the choir class for a couple years. But during my senior year, I had to switch out. I was in an English class that I thought would kill me, and, being the theater kid I was, the Shakespeare English class had an opening that I decided to take. Brenna happened to be in that class too, but that had nothing to do with it. Nothing at all! You don't believe me? Well, neither do I!

The problem was that choir was fourth period, and so was Shakespeare English. Although I couldn't attend the class, I could show up to after school practice and catch up. When I told my choir teacher about the switch, she said she was disappointed because I wouldn't show up to choir practice if I were not taking the class.

I was already a disappointment to her. She didn't even give me a chance to prove myself. She just assumed I would be a lazy disappointment, even when I told her I would come to choir practice. She signed my class-switching form, with her head shaking, and literally walked into her office without saying anything.

Now, that's the way I saw it as a teenager. Looking back now, I'm sure she dealt with empty promises from students all the time. She also spent a ton of time outside of school hours, working with students who were often obnoxious and not always kind. There was no reason for me to take it personally, but I was too stuck in my own world not to.

So what did I do? What any teenager would do. I yelled "You suck!" and I ran out and vandalized the building.

I didn't do that. I knew if I ever wrote a book about it, I would want a better story.

In reality, I showed up to practice. She didn't talk to me. She made it a point to give me her patented glare of disdain in front of everyone before continuing. I'm sure she was thinking, "You think you're funny? You may come once just to be a punk and prove a point, but you won't be back."

That wasn't going to stop me. I showed up for chamber choir auditions. I'll admit that I was partially enjoying the fact that I was defying and annoying her, because what teenager doesn't enjoy that? She would ask for volunteers and I would jump up, and she would roll her eyes. I give her credit for not kicking me out immediately. It gave me hope. Maybe she was starting to believe in me.

Nope. I never got invited to participate in chamber choir. I had not convinced her that I would show up to even more extra choir practice.

So what did I do? I showed up anyway. I didn't get accepted into chamber choir—I just got not kicked out of the room where they held practice for chamber choir. Other kids asked what was going on, and I told them the teacher wanted me there, but she just hadn't said it yet. I shared sheet music with the other students, because somehow the teacher forgot to provide some for me.

Week after week I would show up. I would practice with the main group after school and the chamber choir during lunch. Since I didn't take the class, I would often come surprised by some new music. I started coming to school early to use the choir room, where I would get the sheet music and practice on my own. The teacher's office was in that room, so I was pretty shameless.

One morning, during my solo practice, the teacher passed by me sitting on the piano. She said in passing, "You're a hero."

What??

I'm a hero now? I used to be an annoying, disappointing teenager. But now, I'm saving lives.

This was a huge lesson for me. People don't have fixed ideas about you, and they aren't out to get you. Usually, people are just trying to get by, doing the best they can, and they have to make decisions. Sometimes we get offended because those decisions involve judgments, but you can't live your life without making judgments. It's not personal. The key is to make as kind of judgments as you can, and be open to changing your mind.

Did I say it's not personal? Most of the time, even when people are *intending* to hurt you, it's because of their own insecurities. Just like the pile driver kid that I forgave, people often hurt you because they feel hurt. Imagine the power of looking past their actions to their soul, and being there for them when they need love. In the case of the choir teacher, she didn't intend to hurt me when she said I wouldn't show up. She was disappointed to see me go the way of many of others, making empty promises, and she simply expressed her feelings.

She wasn't perfect in the way she did it, but I don't know if that's because she messed up or because there really is no perfect way to do most things. In the end it motivated me to try harder, so really

I should thank her. Be humble, and admit that you are not perfect, so you can love yourself for being imperfect. Then, when the chance comes to prove someone wrong, you can give it a try without the pressure that you have to win an argument or prove someone wrong. Just be you, and be confident doing your thing.

PROCRASTINATE YOUR LAZINESS

A couple months into writing this book, I had a really rough day, and all I could think to write was the truth of the moment. I share this with you so you understand that this book wasn't written in isolation, as if I was writing about a past life. Life is the same today as it has been, and the act of writing this book is as hard as any accomplishment. In fact, to this day, it's probably the most difficult long-term thing I've done.

This is all I could write that day:

> I really don't feel like working on this book right now. I didn't sleep well last night, and I really needed decent sleep to fully recover from being sick. Instead, I had a cough all night, so not only was I uncomfortable, but I also had to hold in coughs as long as I could because I felt bad every time I coughed and woke up my wife. She has to be up feeding our baby in the middle of the night, and I know my shift starts at her next feeding around 8 am, so there's no chance of sleeping in.
>
> It could be worse.
>
> I'm tired, but I'm well enough to be up and around. I'm not excited about writing, which is hard because I'm writing a motivational book, but I made a schedule that will help me reach my goal, and that means I have to just start at 2 p.m. I had lunch and allowed myself a little Instagram time during lunch hour, but it's time to put my mind and energy

(as imperfect as it is) toward the thing that will make me look back on my day with gladness, knowing I did my best.

I felt very accomplished that day. I've had days where I wrote more and felt less accomplished. Avoiding laziness is really a balancing act. I hate thinking about balance, because I love a clear-cut way of thinking about something that is always right. I often say, "Change your thinking instead of finding balance" (i.e. Don't worry too much or too little about what people think; just make people feel loved). But I haven't figured out how to ignore balance for laziness. There is value in rest, and there is value is work, and I don't know the key to natural balance. So I made a list.

1. LAZINESS COMES FROM NOT KNOWING WHAT YOU REALLY WANT.

If you are starving, it is easy to know what you want: food. If you see food for the first time, and it's a mile away, you will immediately get up and get to that food as fast as you can. This is an example of a natural consequence. No one needs to tell you why you should get up, or how, or what steps to take. Your body just does what it needs to do to get the food. This is different when you are in the kitchen and "can't find anything to eat." You aren't *that* hungry. You don't want to get up for the remote because you don't care *that* much that the channel is changed.

Imagine if you could care about everything you do. Then you would never be lazy. If you have something that you feel you are lazy about, you can find a way to apply natural consequences to it, and naturally you will stop being lazy. It's what people are doing when they set goals that they care about, but it falls apart when you don't actually care about those goals.

For example, I don't care about working out. I wanted to look buff for a second, so I worked out for a week. But I didn't really care if I was buff, so I stopped. I have done this many times, not because I would renew my desire to get buff, but because I knew working out is good for me, and getting buff was the best motivator I could think of. Then I read something about back workouts solving neck problems, and I had neck problems. I was so sick of waking up every day with a sore neck. It was something that actually had a real, negative affect on my life. So I started going to the gym to do back exercises. It was simple and short, just a few exercises, addressing the one real health concern I had. I got into the habit, so it started getting easier. I added chest exercises to balance it out, because otherwise I would cause other problems. It was simple and intrinsically motivated, so I kept doing it. That led to adding other exercises, and I held the longest streak of exercising in my life. It doesn't matter whether or not I'm still doing it. Be motivated by my story! For reals though, eight months is a massive improvement to a week or two.

2. IF YOU GET SICK OF THE THING YOU ARE TRYING, INSTEAD OF QUITTING, FINISH AN INFERIOR VERSION OF IT AS QUICKLY AS POSSIBLE.

You will always regret not fully trying something. In my experience, editing is way easier than building something from the ground up. Especially if you are new to what you are trying, you might just be in that steep learning curve where you have no confidence and you are making tons of mistakes. Everyone goes through that, and you don't get to be amazing at something until you've suffered through being terrible at it.

But don't just quit in the middle of it. Even in writing this book, I have wanted to quit a few times. I would be in the middle of a chapter, feeling like everything I was writing was so terrible, and I couldn't stand the thought of wasting a few more hours trying to get it right. So, instead of getting it right, I would just get it done. This is where Elizabeth Gilbert saved me with "Done is better than good."[14] Once it's done, I can go back and edit later, but the worst thing for a writer is a blank page. I would go back later and read through, finding some gems and throwing out some of the stuff that wasn't working, and I felt so much better that it was getting close to something presentable.

This will teach you what you care about and is an important part of finding your style. If it turns out you care, you'll go back and edit it or redo it. If you don't care, you'll never want to do it again, and you will learn that it doesn't interest you as much as you thought. Give yourself time away from it. Distance makes the heart grow fonder. The grass is greener on the other side, so make it the other side for a while. Either way, don't regret trying it. If nothing else, it will be a souvenir of that time and what you learned, and you can fondly remember how much you never want to do it again.

3. DON'T RUN FASTER THAN YOU HAVE STRENGTH.

This is that balancing part that I don't like to think about. I am terrible at this. My wife will tell you—in fact, she will shout from the rooftops—how terrible I am at this. She is, without a doubt, incredibly annoyed by the fact that I'm writing a book, writing a movie, working on Studio C, building bookshelves for our living room (which she wanted done sooner than I will get them done), and I have her and a daughter to spend time with. Oh, also I'm auditioning for a show where I would have to travel the world for a few weeks. (Awkward teethy smile emoji)

The best way I have found balance is by trial and error. Try something, include self-care, and see how you feel at the end of the day. If you feel like your self-care slipped into laziness, try a little less relaxing the next day. But if you feel like you are still exhausted, isolated, or losing hope (even while being productive), then you need more self-care. It's about avoiding laziness, not avoiding wasting time.

You have to be aware of yourself. When I was sick and could only write that short excerpt about not wanting to write, I felt great about accomplishing what little I could do in my situation. So whether it's physical or mental weakness, or lack of resources or time, or some other factor limiting you, don't sit there pitying yourself. Do what you can and be proud of it.

I love the advice Carl Honoré gives in his book, *In Praise of Slow*. We try to squeeze as much as we can into our time. Instead, we should give time to everything, and do less, and we will be more productive. Our minds will work better when they can relax and focus on fewer things at once, so we end up actually getting more done. Double the time you think you need to do anything. Then start on time, and dedicate your thoughts to that thing, so you can enjoy the doing of it and not feel rushed. There's nothing worse than being in the middle of something and realizing you are late to your next thing, just to never catch up and feel like you aren't doing anything. Cut out as much as you can from your life, and you will be forced to figure out what is most important.

4. DON'T DO WHAT YOU WANT TO DO. DO WHAT YOU WILL WANT TO HAVE DONE.

Does that make sense? Sometimes we don't feel like doing something, but does that mean we shouldn't do it? I've thought a lot about this because I always hear people saying, "Do what you want to do!" But sometimes I just want to sleep. So I came up with this mantra to replace it. Instead of doing what you want to do now, project into the future and look back on your day. Will you be happy at the end of the day if you did it or if you didn't do it? Do what you *will want to have done* when you look back on your day.

I love this concept, because it is the most helpful thing for me to remember in the moment. I may not feel like doing it, but I know the feeling I will get at the end of the day if I do it. And this helps you find balance, because the answer isn't always to do the hard thing. Sometimes you can honestly say to yourself that you have worked hard and you want to enjoy something, because you can look back with regret for not enjoying things just as much as you can regret not doing things. You won't get it perfectly right every time, and that's fine, because it's still trial and error.

The point is that you aren't run by your feelings; you are run by your desires. Some people might call this self-discipline, and it basically is, but my paradigm is more playful and less punitive. Don't discipline (or punish) your current self; reward your future self.

5. IF THINE APP OFFEND THEE, CUT IT OFF.

It is very likely that you have used your phone to waste time that you have regretted wasting. Do not be afraid to delete apps that waste your time! If you feel gross after using an app because you have been MIA for two hours and you got nothing out of it, and your lips are chapped from lack of water, and the person bleeding on the side of the road yelling for help is now dead, stop using that app. To ruin another biblical scripture, "Even so, every good app bringeth forth good fruit; but a corrupt app bringeth forth evil fruit." If it doesn't do you good, it ain't good.

I know I talk about Matt Meese a lot, and usually in a good light, but he suggested a corrupt app to me once. It's called "Adventure Capitalist" and you click a button to pretend to start a business, and then you click a button to pretend to sell stuff, and then you click a button so the computer clicks the button for you. That is the entire game, but for some evil reason, it is so addicting because you see your money go up and up, and you can get upgrades. One upgrade makes you start the whole game over but *this time* it goes a little faster, so you make money faster but you have to do the whole thing again. That way, there's no end in sight, and you keep going back to make sure all the buttons are clicked. There is no skill and it is the devil.

My life changed the day I deleted that app. It was the bravest thing I did that day, and I was finally free. I couldn't keep going into the app to check it, because it wasn't there anymore. You have to actually *delete* the app—you have to commit—or your suffering will never end.

It does not matter how much "work" you put into the app. If it is bad for you, it is bad for you. You can't say, "I put so much work into making this cake out of gun powder and thorns and sin, so I have to eat it now." In economics, it's called "sunk costs" because you can't get your money back (it's sunk), but you can decide not to waste the money you still have on it. Don't keep making a decision you know is bad just because you've already spent a ton of time making it. Let it go—it's in the past—and move forward with better decisions.

Seriously though, delete the app.

6. WHEN YOU DON'T KNOW WHERE TO START, YOU'RE IN THE SAME PLACE AS EVERYONE ELSE. WHEN YOU START ANYWAY, YOU'RE IN THE SAME PLACE AS THE MOST SUCCESSFUL PEOPLE ON EARTH.

Just start! That's all. Next!

7. USE POSITIVE SELF-CONTROL. FILL YOUR TIME WITH GOOD RATHER THAN EMPTYING OUT THE BAD.

Darkness is only the absence of light. Fill a room with light, and the darkness goes away automatically. Fill your life with good things, and the bad goes away automatically.

In *On Balance,* Adam Phillips said, "We tend to think of morality now as more to do with self-control than poise, more about holding back than going forward, more about discipline than about tact."[15] I love the idea that morality itself should be more about creating good than refusing bad. Most religious people I know, including myself, get caught up in what *not* to do. Then religion gets confusing or limiting because you get caught up in what is bad in the world. Instead, focus on the good, and do as much good as you can. You won't have time for the bad, so you don't have to worry so much about it.

We often think of failure as not reaching our goal. Instead, we can think of failure as not having a goal. If I ride my bike ten feet and fall, some would consider that a failure. But I didn't fail, because I got closer to my goal of riding fourteen feet.

The next chapter is about failure, and how great it is, and I can't wait for you to fall in love with failure. So, let's leave laziness behind, because I think the real you wants the dream life, which is the result of working toward great things. It's the kind of life most people don't make because they don't feel like it. E. M. Gray, in his essay "The Common Denominator of Success," said, "[The successful person has] the habit of doing things failures don't like to do." Neither do you most of the time, but now you'll do it anyway.

THIS IS WHAT A FAILURE LOOKS LIKE

It's surprising how much I always enjoyed dating, considering how clueless I was at it.

When I first dated Brenna, I failed a lot. We went on a double date with my friend Tommy and her friend Lindsey. We went to a dance, and I didn't realize until I got there that it was an "all ages" dance. I found out "all ages" pretty much means "every age except yours, so none of your friends will be there." It was a little awkward. The only person there that was my age was Tommy's girlfriend. So, I basically invited Brenna to a dance with old people and little kids and made her friend go with a guy who hung out with his own girlfriend instead of her. I really nailed that one.

Luckily, she agreed to hang out with me again, but for some reason her friend wasn't interested in a double date. We hung out at my house and watched a movie, but I made another mistake. We watched *Saturday's Warrior*, and Brenna wasn't Mormon. This is significant because *Saturday's Warrior* addresses ideas about Mormons that could seem strange to a sixteen-year-old Catholic girl. I was on a roll.

Another time, we went and saw *Napoleon Dynamite*. The classic dinner and a movie was as safe as I could get. What wasn't safe was that I didn't check the gas gauge, and we got stuck on a shady country road in the middle of the night. Eventually a friend came with a gas tank and saved us. My plan to have a date go well, however, could not be saved.

After all this, she kept dating me. No matter how many times I failed, she wanted to be with me. She must have really liked me, and that is exactly what I learned from that. I could give her friend the worst date of her life, show her a movie that emphasized the weirdest parts of my religion, and put her in danger, and she would still want to be with me. It's for the best, because if everything had gone well, I wouldn't know that she would love me in the hard times, or the weird times, and she would probably just marry me because of how hot I am.

FAILURE IS ~~NOT AN~~ *THE ONLY* OPTION

I think people are really afraid of failure. As much as we have all heard that success only comes after failure and that failure is a part of the process, a few encouraging quotes don't change a lifetime of being told you need to succeed as much as possible. What I'm trying to do is help people change their perspective to believing that success doesn't happen in spite of failure; it happens *because of* failure.

Is that crazy? Are you thinking, *Oh James, you're just being overly sensational and saying something crazy to sell books. Everyone knows that eventually to succeed you have to do something right.*

Well, of course that's true. Or is it???

Is it really that you eventually have to do something right? Or just that you have to do *something*? I bet you can't explain to me exactly what it means to do the "right" thing, but I can clearly explain to you what it means to do something. Explanation: just do something.

Doing something perfectly right would mean you have a perfect knowledge of every effect your action will have on everything it touches. It would mean you have the skills to do exactly what is best for everything and everyone involved. But the same thing may be a benefit or handicap depending on the situation. For instance, if I want to build a table, is the right thing to make it big enough for my family, or big enough to host people? Should I make it fancy so it makes my house look good, or cheap to save money because somewhere people are starving? What about a more seemingly obvious example? If two people start fighting, should I stop the fight? What if that means I get involved and I die and my family is left in ruins? Or what if they are professional fighters and I stop the fight and they lose their jobs and *their* families are left in ruins? I couldn't live with myself.

The point is there are too many factors to decide what the right way to do things is in a lot of situations. Yes, there are situations where the answer is easy. Should I slap my dog while reciting the Declaration of Independence? Ninety-nine percent of the time, no, of course not. But you can always do something with the intention of creating good in the world.

The inventor of penicillin was a failure. His plans did not work out, and he didn't accomplish this feat by doing what he set out to do. Penicillin was discovered by accident. But why do we call it an accident instead of a failure? Because "accident" is a word we give to failures once we realize they led to success. If the goal were to kill off the human race with infection, then we would have called this discovery a failure. It's all about perspective.

I actually did make a dining table, and it was a failure. We have used it for the last six years in our house. Our friends have complimented it, and my wife wants to keep it forever. If you showed it to someone who makes dining tables, they would agree that it was a failure. The legs and breadboards are not supported correctly. It doesn't allow for movement due to changes in humidity. The breadboards are therefore sagging instead of being flat. The boards are unmodified 2×4s, and they have a gap between them where food falls that is impossible to clean, because the gaps are just big enough for crumbs to fall in, but just small enough to not let the crumbs out. But did it serve its purpose? Absolutely. And I'm proud of my very first woodworking project.

I love the story on the first page of *Mindset* by Carol Dweck. She was studying the behavior of children solving puzzles.[16] She wanted to understand how they would cope with failure. Of course there were plenty of kids who started crying when they couldn't figure it out, but two of the responses are so great. One kid "rubbed his hands together, smacked his lips, and cried out, 'I love a challenge!'" while another looked up and said, "You know, I was hoping this would be informative!" Cute kids.

At worst, failure can lead to the loss of things that might have been lost anyway. At best, you discover penicillin. You can't be holding on to all those things you have no control over.

We have already talked about how we can't hold on to the things we can't control, because then they will control us. This has to apply with failure too. Because if you say that you had total control over this, then you can't stop there. You have to say you have control over everything your kids do because you "could have" been a better parent. You have to take responsibility for almost everything happening around you because of the long chain of events all stemming back to when you slapped your dog while reciting the Declaration of Independence. And nobody should have to feel bad for doing that *when the situation calls for it.*

We all play a part, so none of us has perfect control. Do what you can to make the world a better place, and no matter how much influence you have on your disappointments, you just can't fully blame yourself. In fact, don't fully blame others either. I've already said I think the world isn't fair, because it is kinder than it is fair. Be kinder than you are fair, especially to yourself.

VULNERABILITY SHMULNERABILITY

We're so afraid of being vulnerable because we think it's the only way for us to fail. In reality, it's the only way for us to succeed. When we put up walls to keep all the enemies out, those same walls keep our friends out too. Don't keep pain and failure out, because you will also keep joy and success out.

Yes, being vulnerable can open you up to failure, because you're trying something that isn't guaranteed to go how you planned. But from now on, I'm changing the definition of failure. No longer does failure mean devastation, hopelessness, or that your life can never be as good as you once thought. Failure means humility and respect for the world as it really is. When you fail, it teaches you what might be wrong with the way you are doing things. Therefore, failure is a quick way to find truth. It's a quick way to find yourself. So, if you are vulnerable, you are not just opening yourself up to failure, you are opening the path to finding yourself.

BEING IS HAPPY,
HAVING IS NOTHING

We worry about a lot of things. We worry that we will be okay, that we will have money, family and friends, health. We worry about whether we are living with purpose, and we read books about it.

Why do we worry about these things? Because there is no guarantee that we will have them. If there were a guarantee, we would have nothing to worry about. When kids are provided for, they never worry about money, because in their world it's just a guarantee that there will be enough. Kids worry as much as adults, but they worry about whether they will get the toy they want, whether their friend will still like them, or whether their parents will get mad at them for misbehaving.

So what do we do? We do everything we can to ensure that we have as close to a guarantee as we can get. The better the job, the *more likely* I will always have enough money. The more I impress people, the *more likely* they will want to be my friend or my coworker. The more I pray, the *more likely* God will give me what I desire.

We get as close as we can to securing these important things, but even then *there is no guarantee*. There are multi-millionaires who lose everything because someone sued them. Nothing they could have done. There are people who lose part, if not all, of their family to tragedy. Nothing they could have done. And the list goes on with all the different things that you can worry about losing, and as hard as you try, you have no guarantee that you will keep any of it, even down to your own life.

So, most of us take whatever strength we have and hold on tight to the things we think we need. We tell ourselves it's the best we can do and if something gets taken from us, then poor us, and shame on them. Shame on people who mistreat us, and shame on the corrupt leaders who don't look out for us, and shame on that guy who flipped me off on the freeway, and shame on God for letting any of it happen. We turn to blame. It's the only explanation for losing the things we hold dear; "Someone ruined my life, and there was nothing I could do about it."

How depressing! That can't be the answer. That mindset gives away all control over your life and your happiness to factors that you can't control. You're being tossed about by the wind, and you have no anchor.

There is a better way: change your perspective from *having* what you need to *creating* what you need.

You can have more than most others and be miserable. You can have less than most and be the happiest person on earth. So it can't be about what you have. We all know materialism doesn't bring happiness in principle, but how much do we apply it to our worries?

In *7 Habits*, Stephen R. Covey talks about the *haves* and the *be's*.[17] Needing the *haves* gives everything else the power to control our lives, because our happiness is dependent on impermanent things. The *be's* come from the inside out, where we have total control, because our happiness is dependent on our own choices.

How much money do you need? Think about how much money you had this year. Could you have done with one less dollar? The answer is yes. What about two? What about three? I certainly could go a while answering yes, and most of you could as well. So, where does it stop? Where is the actual line where you lose the last dollar and you are miserable? Would you be miserable with no money? Maybe, as you ponder every situation, you realize even in the worst-case scenario that family and friends would take care of you. So then you start subtracting dollars from their accounts.

This could go on for a long time. What if we start subtracting friends instead of dollars? How many friends do we *really* need to not be miserable? We can get by on some tiredness, so how much sleep do we need? What about some sickness? How much health do we *really* need? And then, bear with me here, we get down to the basics. How long does my life *really* need to be? Can I be grateful enough that with one last breath of life I think, "At least I have this mome—"

The point is, *what are you so worried about*? If every moment, every friend, and every dollar is just bonus, then why do we worry whether some or all of it will be taken away?

If you're thinking, "If nothing matters, then what's the point of trying at all?" then you're still thinking in terms of having. I'm not saying that nothing matters or has meaning and value. I'm saying the value of your life and the source of your happiness does not depend on whether you have any particular thing to *consume* (or use). It depends more on how you use what you do have to *produce*.

I'm going to use these business-y terms, *consume* and *produce*, because the growth and success of a business is a perfect analogy for your personal growth and success. *Consuming* simply means to use up and is the opposite of *producing*, which means to create more.

Who has more wealth? The person who produces more than they consume. Who has more personal wealth (i.e. happiness, kindness, confidence, etc.)? The person who produces more than they consume. I think these terms express what I'm saying a little better than *having* and *doing*, because *producing* emphasizes building up rather than just *doing* any some random thing, and *consuming* emphasizes using up rather than *having* some random thing. You are always doing one or the other.

You have complete control over what you choose to do. You control whether you gain knowledge or skills, and whether you use those knowledge and skills to create value. You control your own mind. You decide how you look at life and others, and whether you will use your mind to build others up or tear them down (to produce good or consume good). Do you have control over the chemicals in your brain, or whether you feel like doing something good at the moment? No, but you can still choose to do that good thing even when you don't feel like it.

All of a sudden, you're in complete control of your life. Nothing can get you down, because none of the things outside of your control are necessary for your happiness. Your happiness is based solely on what you decide to do. You can decide to smile and give joy to someone else, or to scowl and take joy away (to produce or consume). The great thing is, if you happen to have a bad day and scowl at someone, you aren't ruining anyone's life, because that person also has the ability to choose to replace the joy you stole with joy they produce.

Am I saying you shouldn't consume? Absolutely not. If I have the opportunity to eat a delicious piece of cheese (a literal consumption of food), then I will be glad to enjoy that piece of cheese. The pleasures of life are here for us to enjoy as much as we possibly can. In fact, what's the point of producing so much if no one ever consumes it? *The trouble comes in believing that consuming is more important, or even more joyful, than producing.*

It's just like the old saying goes, "Give a man a fish, he'll consume it. Teach a man to fish, he'll produce more fish." (I might have paraphrased.)

If you are only a consumer, you are completely at the will and whim of those who produce. You have no choices but those that are given to you. If you are a producer, you are a creator. You build things where there was nothing, and you give life where there was death. At any moment, you can just decide to create, and you can do so.

Doesn't that fill you with hope? No longer are you a victim of life's misfortunes. Nothing that happens *to you* has the power to make you miserable. No matter what happens, you can choose misery or happiness. I suggest happiness.

Yay! Life solved, right? It's not that easy. It is simple, but simple is different from easy. If I say, "Get to the top of that mountain and you'll be happy," it's a simple task and you understand how to get it done; it's just a matter of actually doing it. That's harder.

You have to practice the paradigm. So let's practice a little.

Situation 1. You want to consume a pizza. There is no pizza around, but there are ingredients to produce a pizza. What should you do?

Answer 1. Produce a pizza. Okay, so we started simple. I just wanted to warm you up. Ready for a more complicated one? Good. Let's do this.

Situation 2. You are talking with a friend, and you know you want to bring up that you are bothered by how they keep slapping you. When you are about to mention it, they bring up that they are bothered by how you keep kicking them. (You guys have a weird relationship.) You know you care about each other, but you feel a fight coming on (finally, a verbal fight and not a physical fight, which I assume consists of a lot of slapping and kicking). What should you do?

Answer 2. If you think in terms of producing, you want to build something up. In this case, you can build trust. You can either consume trust by asking your friend to listen to you, or you can create trust by fully listening to them first, without excuses, using apologies and kind words to make sure they feel your love. Then, once you have created trust, they will *want* to listen to you. There will be enough trust there that they will be happy to let you consume some of it.

Situation 3. You really want to be an actor, but you didn't get into a play. In other words, someone didn't choose you to consume the opportunity to play that part.

Answer 3. The beautiful thing about producing is there are a million ways to produce, because you're the one creating it, so you design it according to your style however you want. You may not have gotten that *one* opportunity, but you can make any opportunity you want. Put on your own play. It will take more work, but you'll have a way cooler experience to look back on and learn from. You will learn skills that give you the power to produce opportunities for yourself in the future, *and* you'll produce opportunities for others (another beautiful thing about producing). You also don't have to be limited to a play. Maybe you would rather make a movie. Again, write whatever you want, film where and how you want, and give opportunities to whomever you want. You can definitely have just as much fun (I would argue more fun) and you learn more in the process, becoming not just a better actor but a better filmmaker a well.

Situation 4. You want to study math at Harvard, but you didn't get in. What should you do?

Answer 4. First, analyze why it needs to be Harvard, or even why specifically math. Maybe you would be just as happy taking the opportunity to start at your community college. My wife really wanted to study at a university but didn't get into any of the universities she applied to. She was disappointed at first, especially because her best friend got into San Diego State University and she didn't. She ended up going to a junior college. After two years, she transferred to San Diego State University and graduated at the same time as her friend from the same college. You never know where you will end up. In fact, she is a huge proponent of community college, because it allowed her to have time to figure out her major with less pressure and to experience two different colleges. She wouldn't have had it any other way.

If you don't get the opportunity you want, you may not be able to start your own college, but you can produce more proof they should accept you, for instance, by going to a junior college and doing well. You may discover something about yourself that gives you better preparation and a more solid argument for why they should accept you.

When I got my first job after college, they initially told me there was no room for me anymore. This engineering company had interviewed me, but they said their funding situation had changed and they wouldn't be able to hire me. I was bummed, because I was more than a month out of school with an engineering degree, I had no prospects, and I was very interested in the work they were doing there. A few minutes after they told me the news, I called them back. I said that I wanted to learn from them, because I was interested in working in that area, and I would work for them for free. I guess they were impressed with my unorthodox suggestion, so they said I could come in part-time, but they wanted to give me an hourly rate. I was fine with that. I was able to show them who I was and how I worked, and even though I was far behind everyone else in skill, they liked having me as part of the team. After only a couple months, they offered me a full-time position, and that's how I got my first grownup job. I produced an opportunity by offering something unexpected, and luckily it worked out.

Do you know the story of Joseph and the Amazing Technicolor Dream Coat? The Bible also did a version of it. Basically, Joseph was hated by his brothers, thrown into a pit, and sold into slavery. Potiphar, who purchased him, was so impressed with him that he made him his right-hand man. He made an opportunity where there was none, by being genuine, humble, and brave. Then Potiphar's wife framed him, and he was in jail for years, but eventually interpreted Pharaoh's dreams and became ruler of Egypt. Again, he made an opportunity where there was none.

I'll end this chapter with one of Aesop's fables about the goose with the golden egg. A guy finds out that his goose lays golden eggs, and he gets very excited, obviously. He starts to use those eggs to buy bigger and nicer things, until his standard of living is so high that his goose can't keep up. He kills the goose and gets the eggs from inside, but of course there is only one egg ready to go, so it becomes his last golden egg, and he loses everything.

That guy is so stupid. I thought that even when I heard that as a young child. Why would you trade a steady income stream for one day's bonus? Yet we do this all the time. In our relationships, we might continue a fight with a friend to have one golden egg of being right instead of enjoying daily golden eggs from their continued friendship. In school, we might spend another hour playing a game (that we can always play later) instead of finishing our homework so that we can have a great education that will benefit us for a lifetime. We might buy something we can't afford on credit, for the tiny golden egg of having it now, only to lose a lot more money paying interest. We might eat something unhealthy to feel good for a few seconds but feel terrible later.

It goes back to that idea I shared earlier about getting by with as little as possible, whether with money, relationships, taste, time, or anything else we might consume. Invest in these things, instead of just consuming. When you invest, you still use something up, but more comes back to you later. Instead of using your positive energy to tell yourself how pretty you are, compliment someone else and get a compliment *and* a friend in return. Instead of eating only frozen chimichangas because it's cheap and easy, eat good food and your body won't stop working prematurely.

Having means nothing. Creating means everything. *Mabuti tubig* means "good water" in Tagalog, which I think is funny.

NO PAIN, NO BRAIN

Pain or discomfort is necessary for growth. The best thing you can do is shift your paradigm to enjoy pain, or at least appreciate it. Pain is the "hard" of "play hard," and it gives life meaning. There must be opposition in all things so we can enjoy the good in contrast with the bad.

When I was in Divine Comedy, we did a retreat every semester at a place called Spring Haven. It was a big cabin in the mountains with a basketball court, ping-pong tables, and pool tables, and we would bring a ton of snacks. It was so fun and we would always look forward to it.

I remember the feeling of the first time I went. I was so busy doing school and work, and I almost never got a day off. When I got there, I was running around like a little kid all night. I played every game and had a great time. I got hit in the head playing volleyball, so I knew I was on the right track in life. We played murder in the dark, which is amazing in a huge cabin with ten large rooms. Then we stayed up way too late eating and talking, and I couldn't believe I was friends with the most fun people in the world.

I distinctly remember feeling like that break from hard work made it so much sweeter. I made sure to get everything done before we went up, and I had no worries. There were a couple times I went up to Spring Haven, but I had been lazy that week—I knew I had deadlines looming, and I didn't feel like I had done much that week. As much fun as the trips always were, I wasn't able to enjoy that one nearly as much because it wasn't contrasted with working hard and earning the ability to play in peace. I didn't work hard, so I couldn't play hard. If

I had had the mindset to look at my work as play, I could have played hard to get my work done, then played less hard and just enjoyed it. Regrets.

You have probably heard of the book *Man's Search for Meaning*, by Victor Fankl,[18] because it's an incredible story. No one can talk about the value of suffering like a man who was in a concentration camp. Like millions of other Jews during World War II, he was stolen, enslaved, imprisoned, degraded, overworked, and abused. Somehow, he had an incredible strength in his paradigm for meaning and even joy in an insanely terrible situation.

Frankl developed a mindset to find meaning even in the moment of his suffering. He would imagine himself in the future teaching his students the lessons he was learning *as he was getting tortured*. In moments of great distress, he would project himself into the future and use the power of hope to choose how his experience would affect him. Instead of choosing bitterness, which is our natural response to pain, he chose gratitude. He said that this gave him more freedom than his captors. They may have had more liberty—the ability to choose their environment—but he had more freedom—internal power over his personal experience.

He said, "He who has a *why* to live for can bear almost any *how*." I have to take time to calm myself down when someone tells me I'm annoying. I get too angry when something takes too long and delays my plans. I feel so pathetic when I think of this man and his experience.

Can we just embrace that we are a little pathetic and talk about a pathetic example because we all experience it? Do you get frustrated waiting in line? I do. But why is waiting so terrible? I think it's because we have no choice, no power to make things go faster. We are stuck in line and we can't do anything about it. It's like the really pathetic version of not having liberty, like Frankl said. But we still have freedom; we always have power over our personal experience.

Another story that inspires me, baffles me actually, is the experience of Elizabeth Smart. She was kidnapped and she was raped for nine months, and she has somehow found light in the darkest of situations. What she said puts every trial I've ever had into perspective.

"Nobody is trial-free, but we have a choice," she said. "We can choose to allow our experiences to hold us back, and to not allow us to become great or achieve greatness in this life. Or we can allow our experiences to push us forward, to make us grateful for every day we have and to be all the more thankful for those who are around us."[19]

She not only said that we can get past pain, but that pain can push us forward. It makes us more grateful for what we have. She has a better excuse than anyone to choose bitterness, but she knows it would only hurt her. She said, "The best punishment I could give him [her captor] is to be happy." By the way, her book is better than mine, so you probably should have read that instead.

Remember that it took time and perspective, and she mentioned a lot of prayer, to be able to embrace this positive mindset about it. Even then, she has bad days where all that perspective and positive thinking feels far away. It's okay if it is hard to get there. It's okay if your trials make you feel "broken beyond repair" as she did. Her message is hope in the worst of situations and eventual gratefulness even for the pain.

Pain isn't always something that happens to you. Some of the hardest choices to make are the ones where you create the pain.

Anonymous, one of the smartest people on the internet, once said, "If you don't sacrifice for what you want, what you want becomes the sacrifice." My dad always said that the best definition for sacrifice was "giving up something good for something better." You have to make conscious choices to do hard things, or else you will soon lose your ability to make choices, because strength and opportunities only come to those who are prepared for them. You can either choose your pain and create strength, or wait around for the pain that comes from weakness. That wasn't anonymous. That's my own quote. And you can quote me on that!

When you start a difficult project, or reach for a difficult goal, expect it to be difficult to the end. Not only will it be difficult, but also it will be more complicated than you thought. Things always take longer or require more skill than you thought. *But don't give up!* This is where you go from ordinary to extraordinary. From my experience, difficult things always seem like they will never get done. Difficult (a.k.a. worthwhile) things tend to come together at the last minute.

The title for this book didn't come together until the last day, after a month of stressing over it. I had to come up with an idea for a movie, and I came up with five. That would seem like enough, right? I had one day left, and I thought I should really give it everything and see if I could come up with one more. That last idea was the one that was chosen, and now I have an opportunity to write a movie for a major production company. That wouldn't have happened if I didn't give it everything I had until the last moment.

Anything we obtain too easily, we esteem lightly. That is absolutely true. We see rich people, with far more than we have, that don't care about that $5000 jacket they wore once. We see popular people ignore friends that are only there because of popularity. If you get it easily, you just don't care that much about it.

Don't be afraid of pain. Remember to go at your own pace, but don't be afraid to up your game a little and see how far you can go.

NOTES

1. Ed Catmull, *Creativity, Inc.: Overcoming the Unseen Forces That Stand in the Way of True Inspiration* (New York: Random House, 2014).
2. Stephen R. Covey, *The 7 Habits of Highly Effective People: Powerful Lessons in Personal Change* (New York: Free Press, 2004).
3. *The Portable Thoreau*, ed. Carl Bode (New York: Penguin Books, 1982), 342–3.
4. Jim Carrey, *Oprah Show*, aired October 12, 2011 on OWN.
5. Jim Carrey, "Full Speech: Commencement Address at the 2014 MUM Graduation," 11:40, https://www.youtube.com/watch?v=V80-gPkpH6M.
6. Deepak Chopra, *The Seven Spiritual Laws of Success: A Practical Guide to the Fulfillment of Your Dreams* (Amber-Allen Publishing and New World Library, 1994).
7. Carrey, "Full Speech," 23:24, emphasis added.
8. Alfred Binet, *Modern Ideas about Children* (Suzanne Heisler, 1984).
9. Carol S. Dweck, *Mindset: The New Psychology of Success* (New York: Ballantine Books, 2006).

10. Brad Bird, dir., *The Incredibles*, Walt Disney Pictures and Pixar Animation Studios, 2004.

11. Susan David, "The Gift and Power of Emotional Courage," presented November 2017 at TEDWomen, TED video, 10:07, https://www.ted.com/talks/susan_david_the_gift_and_power_of_emotional_courage.

12. Ibid., 9:36.

13. Twenty One Pilots, "Stressed Out," *Blurryface*, Fueled by Ramen, 2015.

14. Elizabeth Gilbert, *Big Magic* (New York: Riverhead Books, 2015).

15. Adam Phillips, *On Balance* (New York: Farrar, Straus and Giroux, 2010).

16. Dweck, *Mindset: The New Psychology of Success*, 3.

17. Covey, *The 7 Habits*.

18. Victor E. Frankl, *Man's Search For Meaning* (Boston: Beacon Press, 1992), 37, http://www.fablar.in/yahoo_site_admin/assets/docs/Mans_Search_for_Meaning.78114942.pdf.

19. Stephanie Grimes, "Elizabeth Smart: 'The best punishment I could give him is to be happy,'" KSL, April 11, 2012, https://www.ksl.com/index.php?nid=148&sid=19942794&title=elizabeth-smart-the-best-punishment-i-could-give-him-is-to-be-happy.

End

Just like introductions, end-of-book summaries are hard for me, because I know they're just going to repeat everything they've already said, and I have major ADHD. If I didn't get it by now, I probably won't get it from a summary. But if you want closure, I'll just say a few things.

Relax about your future. You are going to be okay. You could make the most perfect plans in the world, and they still wouldn't turn out that way. Just make the best plan you can come up with and get started, then let life take you by surprise. Be ready for those surprises by using every day to discover what you love about yourself, and then use those surprises to continue to discover yourself.

If journeying is something you love to do, then life is a journey. Life is a game, if it works for you to think about it that way. Life is a garden. Life is a hacky sack, if anyone is still into that. All that matters is that life is truly *yours*.

Remember you are not becoming something you need to become; you already are everything you need to be. You get to have joy in discovering yourself by gaining knowledge and experience from experimentation and play. That's how I live my life, and it works great for me, so I hope something in this book works for you.

And if nothing in this book is helpful to you, and you still don't know what to do, just remember that most people don't drink enough water every day. You're probably just dehydrated.

Acknowledgments

First, I have to acknowledge my wife, Brenna. I know I already dedicated the book to her (and June, and maybe more kids), but she did more for me while writing this book than anyone, and she is always supportive of my work. Thank you for the nights you took care of June so I could write, not knowing if this would lead to anything other than a few copies of my book on our shelves. Thank you for being proud of me and telling me to be proud of myself. Thanks for being ride or die. Thanks for being you.

Thanks to the English language, without which I never could have written this book.

My parents are the best around. Thanks for always telling me I could do anything. Thanks for making me. Thanks for telling me you're proud of me, even when it's something insignificant like building subpar bookshelves or eating brussels sprouts. Like father, like Jimbo.

Thanks to alarm clocks, without which I wouldn't know I was late.

Thanks to my friends throughout my life for being nice to me even though I was/am definitely weird, stupid, and wrong most of the time.

Thanks to Amy Hackworth, who gave me great notes on my book.

I'd like to thank the Academy and my director.

Thanks to Cedar Fort for wanting to publish this.

Thanks to God, for also making me and for making all the things and people and places that make life beautiful.

And thanks to the real heroes: teachers, farmers, Thor, and Elon Musk.

About the Author

James Perry likes whipped cream—the real stuff, not the spray stuff. He is best known for his work as an actor and writer for the sketch comedy show Studio C. His bachelor's degree in mechanical engineering at BYU took him 5.5 years, because he wasn't smart enough to do it in 4 years. James wants world peace. Until then, he hopes to help people feel peace in their personal lives and realize how great they are. He is the luckiest father and husband to June and Brenna, respectively. He hopes you have a great day.

Scan to visit

www.jamesperryactor.com